*Want To Learn How To Become Wealthy
And Enjoy It?*

This is the book you have been waiting for.

At last — a short, easy, to-the-point hand-book showing you step-by-step how you can *think* wealthy and *become* wealthy. *Think Wealth* is unique in that it takes you through the nitty-gritty yet fun process of *moving you from Thinking* about money to *Doing* about money to where you *Have Money!*

These ten condensed, power-packed lessons guide you on to a new wealthier, happier you.

Here are the proven secrets of Dr. Tag Powell's *Think Wealth Seminars,* which have brought wealth to people across the globe.

And a special bonus — instructions for making your own audiocassette for instant reinforcement at the Alpha brain frequency!

Here, in easy steps, is the way to formulate and attain your goals. Now you can become wealthy by merely changing your attitude and by...

Putting Your Money Where Your Mind Is!

AUDIOCASSETTES BY
DR. TAG POWELL
Think Money Action Kit
Instant Money
Speed Learning Action Kit
Instant Learning
Secrets of Visualization Action Kit
The Silva Method of Mind Mastery
    8-Audiocassette Album
Silva Master Keys Series
    8-Audiocassette Album
Super Subliminals Plus
    8-Audiocassette Album

OTHER BOOKS BY
DR. TAG POWELL
Money and You
As You Thinketh (with James Allen)
Silva Mind Mastery for the 90's
    (with Dr. Judith Powell)
Slash Your Mortgage In Half
How to Develop Your Child's Psychic Abilities
    (with Carol Howell Mills)
Visualization: Health, Wealth and Happiness

THINK WEALTH...
Put Your Money
Where Your Mind Is!

By Dr. Tag Powell

TOP OF THE MOUNTAIN PUBLISHING
Largo, Florida 34643-5117 U.S.A.

THINK WEALTH...
    Put Your Money Where Your Mind Is!
    Copyright 1991, Dr. Tag Powell
The material contained within this book has been re-searched and proven successful in Dr. Powell's "Money & You," "Instant Money," and "Think Wealth" Seminars personally conducted around the world since 1979.

Library of Congress
Cataloging in Publication Data
Powell, Tag.
THINK WEALTH...
    : put your money where your mind is! / by Tag Powell
        p. cm.
Includes bibliographical references
ISBN 1-56087-011-7 (quality pbk) : $6.95
1. Finance, Personal. I Title.
HG179.P59 1991
332.024—dc20   91-11420 CIP

TOP OF THE MOUNTAIN PUBLISHING
11701 South Belcher Road, Suite 123
Largo, Florida 34643-5117 U.S.A.
SAN 287-590X - FAX (813) 536-3681
PHONE (813) 530-0110

ACKNOWLEDGMENTS

To Peggy Paul, a courageous spirit and an open heart, for all her help lo those many years ago. To my editors: my wonderful wife Dr. Judith Powell and editor Yvonne Fawcett.

To Mike and Lou Tannen, Artie Jackerson and Sy Sussman for guiding my early years. Mike taught me to look for the good in everyone and always work in a light of fairness for all; Lou taught me to understand the difference between business and friendship; Artie taught me the work ethic, and; Sy taught me to view each day with interest and humor.

OPTIMAL READING

The type-style, size, column width, and line spacing have been tested at the Speed Reading Institute, Florida, and have been proven to be the most effective for optimal reading speed and comprehension.

TABLE OF CONTENTS

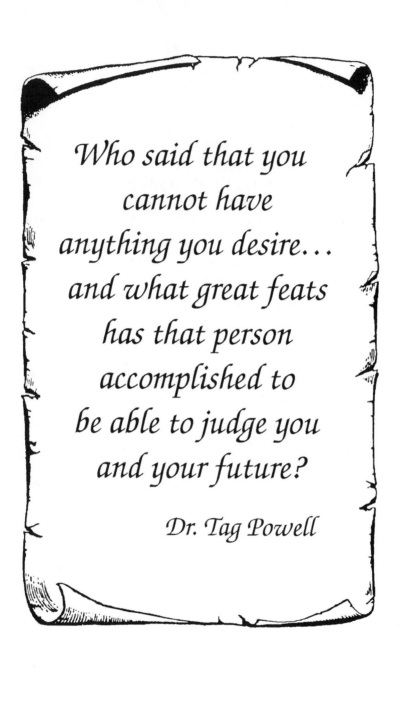

Who said that you cannot have anything you desire… and what great feats has that person accomplished to be able to judge you and your future?

Dr. Tag Powell

HOW TO QUICKLY MIND YOUR MONEY AND ENJOY IT

Are you the one who said that you can't become wealthy? Why not? Today there is a millionaire made every minute of every day. What is the new millionaire's secret? If you had the many hours, weeks or even months to observe and find out why any one individual is successful, you would discover many secrets the wealthy have mastered.

The monied ones may have hit upon these secrets by chance, through trial and error, by sweat and tears — or perhaps by attending one of my *Think Wealth Seminars.* Contained in these ten easy lessons are the patterns of success that the wealthy have used to get wealthier... and now, *you* can model their success.

You don't need money to begin, or even have any previous money success. All you need is a true desire to enjoy a wealthier, healthier and more productive life. Apply the simple steps in this book today and every day... and you will be on your way to quickly becoming wealthier and wealthier. The only requirements are pen and paper — or better still, a spiral-bound notebook. Keep your notes for a permanent record — create your own *Think Wealth Notebook.*

You Control A Multi-Billion Dollar Potential

It has often been stated that your brain functions very much like a computer. The brain\biological computer metaphor with a few adjustments makes a good working model to understand how to gain better control over your potential.

A computer processes and accesses any information stored within. It does not matter if this is correct or incorrect information — and your biocomputer brain does the same thing: it regulates the decisions you make in life based on stored information (memory). Whether the decision is to take a chance on a bowl of chili, to invest in the stock market or to start a new relationship, this regulator helps you decide if an idea is folly or opportunity.

Notice the phrase "helps you decide," for there is another factor which comes into play — the MIND. Science has little hard data on the mind. Much is known about the physical attributes of the brain, but the location and workings and physical dimensions of the mind remain a mystery.

Without getting into philosophy, it might be said that *the mind controls the brain, and the brain controls the body.* That is, the mind controls the brain through thoughts (images); and the brain controls the body through chemical and electrical impulses.

The mind is what controls the creative and logical (thinking) functions of the brain, intuitively analyzing *new* data in a broader light. Some of the control handles are in the realm of consciousness — that state when we are *aware* of what we are thinking. Yet most thought functions are on an inner conscious (automatic) level, or what was formerly called the "subconscious." The mind relies, to a large extent, on the brain for its stored experiences and information. The mind then accesses this information automatically and continuously, much of the time with the individual being unaware.

Most of your money and wealth problems are based on the fact that your *data banks* (brain) store false or incomplete information. Therefore, when your mind accesses the brain's stored information, in making decisions or solving problems about your future, the mind receives incomplete or inaccurate information. However, with the application of the principles in this book *you* can change this automatic cycle.

Brainwave Patterns

The closest thing to being able to measure the mind's output (thoughts) may be to measure brainwave frequencies (electrical impulses). Scientist Dr. Hans Berger, in the 1930's, discovered that the brain pulses with electrical discharges in specific rhythmic patterns. Today, with the use of a machine called an electroencephalograph, we can measure with great accuracy this brainwave activity. While the electrical discharges are a function of the physical brain, the rhythm or flow seems to be controlled by thought or a type of thought-processing — *the mind.*

To further explain the brain/mind relationship: We spend most of our waking hours with a brainwave pattern of about 20 cycles per second (cps), a rhythm science calls a *Beta* brainwave frequency. This pattern changes when we get a flash of insight. The instant a new thought or idea comes to consciousness, our brainwave frequencies slow to approximately ten cycles per second, called *Alpha.* As we go to sleep, our brain rhythm slows from twenty cycles — Beta, and enters the Alpha level between fourteen and seven cycles per second. As we go deeper asleep we enter *Theta* (seven to five cycles per second), and then on to *Delta* which is from five to one cps. During our sleeping hours, we then cycle back up to Alpha or low Beta. Our brain rhythm cycles up and down four or five times a night depending how long we stay asleep.

Science has been able to determine certain mental and physical functions at specific brainwave frequency. As an example: at Beta we do math and most logical processing; at Alpha we do creative, intuitive processing, dreaming and day dreaming. Research has proven that the brainwave pattern called

Alpha, *when controlled with conscious aware-
ness,* becomes the doorway to enter into interaction with the brain/mind processing. This
becomes an intuitive/analytical partnership
— a partnership of Alpha and Beta.

With the proper keys we can unlock the
door to negative, self- defeating stored data in
the inner consciousness so that we can
reprogram or *RE-MIND* at Alpha — thereby
making lasting changes in our behavior and
inner "core" beliefs.

Who's The Matter With Your Computer?

The computer trade uses the term
"GIGO": garbage in — garbage out. One gets
out of the computer exactly what one puts into
the computer... GIGO. To simplify and apply
it to your biocomputer: You begin at birth with
a new "computer," clean and ready for
programming (the in-putting of information).
As you begin to experience life, you (and individuals around you) begin to program your
computer. As you construct your personal
working model of the world, you build your
beliefs and behavior patterns. And these are
the motivations behind your every act.

During the great "ingesting period," you can become "overloaded"... so you develop strategies or *filtering systems* in which you select and retain certain experiences as your "reality" and also reject other experiences which do not easily pass through your "filters." Some knowledge/experiences "do not compute," so they are rejected — filtered out as if they never existed. As you grow, you continue to absorb the experiences/data from others which are input into your computer as "truth"... truth as *they* see it. Frequently this new "second party" information is distorted, inaccurate, and prejudiced by the ignorance or the negative experiences of the giver.

Whether you like it or not, true or false, your brain automatically accepts, as your own, the *attitudes* and *opinions* of others. You accept as your reality the filtered experiences of the people you love and respect: parents, ministers, teachers, friends. This is the *basis for your beliefs*, your "knowledge" of the world, and most importantly... *your inner picture of yourself and your abilities*. This is all on an inner conscious automatic level: you are "stuck" with this type of programming — until you *consciously* decide to change it.

How To RE-MIND Yourself...
The Reprogramming Of New Information

If we GIGO our computer with false input, such as two-plus-two equals five, we will get the same information out each time we enter the two-plus-two math problem.

Look at YOUR programming. What early programs are YOU stuck with? What "computer tapes" are you playing each day? What wealth opportunities are you rejecting because of your limiting filters?

Part or all of your financial problems may be the fact that you don't *think* wealthy. Your first level of change will be, to paraphrase Rene Descartes, "I think, therefore I am" —

> I THINK WEALTHY,
> THEREFORE I AM.

Making The Change Alphamatically

Your biocomputer handles automatic bodily functions — your heart beat, breathing, circulation, digestion. It also handles your learned functions, which I term *Alphamatic* skills — such as walking, tying your shoes, driving a car, hitting a tennis ball, multiplication tables, ad infinitum.

All these learned Alphamatic functions begin at the outer conscious level of mind (*Beta* brainwave). Through logical processing and constant repetition, they eventually are turned over to the inner conscious level of mind (*Alpha* brainwave), and become *Alphamatic.* Your thoughts about wealth and success can be accessed and easily changed at the Alphamatic level. If these thoughts are false or incomplete, they can be reprogrammed — RE-MINDED.

Alphamatic Reprogramming

The visualization training exercise in "Lesson Ten" will give you the *key* to quickly reprogram your biocomputer. This Alphamatic reprogramming goes right to the inner conscious, and can make the changes by simply over-riding years of negative programming. This process of Alphamatic RE-MINDING will give instant results, easily and enjoyably. It will contribute many benefits to your health — with increased ability to cope with daily stress and debilitating problems.

At last, you are on the true road to becoming wealthy, and you will be able to enjoy your new-found riches. But, before you can begin to RE-MIND your money thoughts in order to reach your goals, you must first discover which thoughts are to be Re-minded.

Quick Action Plan To Put Your Money
Where Your Mind Is

This ten-step program — if followed conscientiously *and* consistently — will change your MONEY LIFE.

STEP ONE. Read through this entire book. This will give you an understanding of the principles. Have pen and paper ready to do the exercises as you go. It would be best if you buy a notebook just for your exercise comments so you can periodically review your progress — your *Think Wealth Notebook.*

STEP TWO. Read and practice the Alphamatic programming techniques. Utilize the bonus script (see "Lesson Ten") by recording your own *Alphamatic audiocassette,* to start you on your way.

STEP THREE. Review Lessons One and Two, and practice the ideas given for a full week...while using the Alphamatics from Lessons One and Two (positive thoughts for RE-MINDING) at a relaxed level of mind (Lesson 10) two or three times daily.

STEP FOUR. Review Lesson Three, and practice these ideas for a full week. Add the ideas to Lessons One and Two, and continue using the Alphamatics (Lesson 10)...adding the newer Alphamatics...two or three times each day.

STEP FIVE. Review Lesson Four...and add to Lessons One, Two and Three. Use the Alphamatics from Lessons One through Four two or three times daily.

STEP SIX. Study Lesson Five... review Lessons One, Two, Three and Four. Continue with the Alphamatic programming.

STEP SEVEN. Study and put into practice the suggestions given in Lesson Six. Review your understanding of the first five lessons... and continue using the Alphamatics.

STEP EIGHT. Study and put into practice the suggestions given in Lesson Seven.

Review your understanding of the first six lessons... and continue using the Alphamatics.

STEP NINE. Study and put into practice the suggestions given in Lesson Eight. Review your understanding of the first seven lessons... and continue using the Alphamatics.

STEP TEN. Study the concepts taught in Lesson Nine, and begin to put these to work in your daily activities. Reinforce the lessons learned throughout this book... and *concentrate* on a different Alphamatic each day. You are now ready to Put Your Money Where Your Mind Is!

Be sure to drop me a note in care of the Publisher to share your successes!

Dr. Tag Powell

HOW TO THINK WEALTHY

What! You don't think wealthy? I'm not surprised. If you are like most of us, you also don't believe you were BORN wealthy. For years you have been programmed by the negative and potential-limiting beliefs of your family and friends. You have most likely accepted *their comfort zone (their belief systems about money)* as your own. They have helped you build walls that keep you *in your place.*

Our *comfort zones* are internal pictures of ourselves. All actions and ideas are compared to this internal pattern. Our *filters* are the doorways created to guard this inner picture. These filters can block, distort our desire for something we have never had or done before. A new idea gets compared to previous experiences and data (beliefs). If the new thought is outside our comfort zone, a warning flag goes up in our inner conscious...a flag that warns this new pattern is *not like us.*

Anything outside our comfort zones will cause stress. Our inner conscious will put blocks in the way of this new goal in order to keep us "safe." Our inner conscious will create an uneasy feeling, an insecurity and build fear. Remember fear can be defined as *F.E.A.R...*"False Evidence Appearing Real." Unless this stress to the *new you* is diverted, it will lead to ill health. To keep healthy and successful we must adjust this Internal Comfort Zone.

In order to change, you will want to look at some of those old instilled programs... to expand your comfort zone to encompass more of life. The next step will be to eliminate any old ideas which are *nonfunctional* — your excess baggage. A thorough job of *Mental House Cleaning* will speed you on your way to the top: to a fuller, healthier and wealthier life.

From birth your data processing has been accelerated. As you grow the world becomes your teacher. Every moment is packed with new learning experiences. You use all of your five senses to input data into your brain. You use sight, sound, smell, touch and taste to expand your information.

Perhaps a scenario such as this happened to you. Think back.... You are a very small child and your favorite uncle gives you a bright new shiny coin. You see the newness, the way it sparkles as it reflects the light. As you take this marvelous coin in your hands, you feel its edges. You wonder what it tastes like. You put the coin into your mouth... it's cool... has an unusually tangy taste... it.... Suddenly, a sharp scream brings you out of your reverie. It's your mother's voice — a tone you hear when something is wrong. You sense danger. She is saying, "Take that out of your mouth! That money is dirty! You don't know where that's been!" And it is at that moment that you may have started your earliest program (belief) about money.

At this early stage your computer for the most part is blank, wide open. And everything goes in to form your future — your comfort or UNcomfort zone that will rule your life. How does the above scenario make such an impact? Let's take the phrase, "Money is dirty." You are taught to keep clean; to stay away from anything that will soil you. Your parents always get angry when you get dirty. And a child is constantly seeking parental approval. At the inner conscious level, since money is dirty, your mind will help keep you far away from that filthy lucre. Therefore, you will stay "clean," and your parents will approve. And you will stay poor...or just "getting by."

Who's The Matter With Your Money?

Who is keeping you poor? *Whose thoughts* are you thinking when you think about money? On the inner level we learn from and accept the programs which flow through our personal filters. There are three types of programs that easily get through our filters:

1. Thoughts and ideas from people we love and respect.

2. A thought that is continuously repeated.

3. Thoughts that match or support previously stored data.

Most of us learn first from the people in our environment. We BUY into their belief systems. We are taught the "truth" as they know it, and if their "truth" was poverty, or slightly better, this becomes our reality. Have you ever noticed that the children of the wealthy become wealthy in their own right? The children of the rich have a *wealth belief struc-*

ture. They are brought up with a different "truth."

Money is a popular topic of conversation, but rarely is anything nice said about it. You grow up hearing and processing all sorts of information regarding money. Your parents were the "big" people who "knew" everything. When others would say similar things about money your mentors would nod and smile knowingly. You heard and processed this also. Because you repeatedly heard the *Neggi's* (negative or limiting statements), they were absorbed through your filters, and are now stored in your brain. Other corresponding negative thoughts can then easily flood in because the patterns have been set, the pathways have been made. Your mental defenses filter out anything that is "not like you." And in the case of stored false ideas regarding money, any time you have a chance to make money or to win something, your brain accesses: "I never win anything... You have to work hard for your money... It takes money to make money... Rich people aren't happy.

You've probably heard and possibly used programs/expressions like: "Poor, but happy," "Poor, but honest," "Poor baby," or "Filthy rich." You received these and many other negative programs day after day... and these

Neggies

helped to set your present attitude and beliefs about money.

Are You A Poverty Promoter...
Without Knowing It?

How do you feel about money? Are you always commenting about the high cost of things? Do you begrudge paying your honest debt? What are YOUR expressions? Do they reflect your money consciousness? Do they keep you poor?

Do you really believe that prices are high? Using the techniques I've written in this book has given me the opportunity to travel around the globe. I have become aware that throughout the world, wages never seem to be at an equal level with costs. However, somehow we do seem to keep pace with our economy. Realize that you probably live better or at least equal to most individuals living on this planet, and in most cases, better than at any other time period in history.

The United Stated of America is "a great buy" in any language. In this country almost everyone owns the same category of things as the very wealthy. You have a car, a phone, a TV, a VCR, and probably have, or someday will have, your own home. These are things we take for granted in our land of plenty. It may help you to remember that in many countries people only dream about these luxuries. For example, in Russia there is only one car for every forty-five people... try that in your car pool!

So you see, your statements about a poor chance for riches in your country are not only negative, they are false — the statements of a loser, a Poverty Promoter.

> The loser complains; the winner makes the best of a situation.

How To Become A Prosperity Promoter

Let us look at those negative expressions, clearly and honestly. It has often been said that, "Money can't buy happiness." If this limiting statement is in your biocomputer... whenever you have extra money or when things are looking up in the money department... you will find that you won't feel happy, you'll feel unsatisfied. And, since your mind knows that you want to be happy, it will steer you as far away as possible from having substantial money. Now, think that *with money you can certainly look for happiness in some interesting places!*

Money still can't buy happiness, *but with money you can rent it long enough so you think you own it!*

Even the most quoted statement, "Money is the root of all evil," is a misquote. The original statement is, "The LOVE of money is the root of all evil," and that really was meant as the love of money *above all other things.* We might say that *the LACK of money is the root of all evil.*

It is also well to RE-MIND yourself that: It's not "dirty money." You were taught to stay clean... and were reprimanded or punished when you got dirty. You didn't like to be yelled at, so you stayed as clean as possible. If you have this negative statement ingrained in your brain, there is an equation in your mind: MONEY = DIRTY!

DIRTY IS BAD
MONEY IS DIRTY
MONEY IS BAD

You must keep away from dirt... therefore, you must keep away from money. And that is what your mind helps you do — keep out of arms reach of money. Now, think that it's okay — *you can be spic and span and wealthy too.*

"Money doesn't grow on trees." This is my *favorite* negative statement because EVERYONE has heard it when they were young (and are possibly still staying it as an adult!) What this statement is really saying is that it is hard to come by money. Therefore, since your inner conscious believes it, you find that you have to work hard for your money. Nothing is as easy as it seems. Now, think that *money grows everywhere that you plant the seed.*

It's not true that, "It takes money to make money." Look at all those people who accomplish much with just a dream. *It only takes thought to make money.* All you have to do is set your mind to it, and you are now learning to *put your money where your mind is!*

Negative statements are keeping you in a rut (a rut is a grave with the ends kicked out)! Take action NOW! Start to clear out your *Neggi's,* those self-defeating statements. Now is the time to do your own *Mental House Cleaning.* Become aware and clean out all negative garbage statements. Ask yourself, "Is this a statement of a poverty promoter, or is it a statement of a winner?" Take the following steps NOW and be on the road to good fortune.

Cancel The Poverty Statements
In Your Computer

Do you tell yourself these Neggi's: "Money is the root of all evil"..."Money doesn't grow on trees"..."It takes money to make money?"

STEP A. Take a pen in hand, and turn to a blank page in your *Think Wealth Notebook*. Draw a line down the center from top to bottom. On the left hand side of the line write the above poverty statements — and any more that you can remember. Take your time and think of all the Neggi's; the negative statements about money that you have heard or said yourself. Don't fluff this off as unimportant. It is essential to recall your Neggi's — remember GIGO. If you can recall them, they have made an impression on your brain neurons. And they are affecting your ability to make money!

If any of these expressions are used in your vocabulary, even in jest, make a promise to yourself to never use them again. If you find any negative money expressions being said by you or to you, say aloud the words "Cancel, Cancel" to mentally cancel the thought, then replace it with a positive, money-enhancing thought which should also be said aloud (see Step B). *Be sure to date your notebook page.*

You will want to keep an on-going record —
that you will review to see your progress. Periodically repeat this exercise. After you have
made a very careful study of your negative
thoughts, and written them down, move on
to...

Creating A Positive Prosperity
Promotion Statement

STEP B. IN INK, to the right of that line,
across from each of your negative statements... write a positive replacement: a
Prosperity Promotion statement. This positive replacement statement can now be used
in place of the negative one — a positive statement you can have fun using, all the while
reprogramming and widening your positive
money belief (comfort zone). When you are
satisfied with a positive replacement statement — draw a line through each corresponding Neggi. It is CANCELED.

Don't overlook the importance of this
process. If you have done a thorough *Mental
House Cleaning* in Step B, the next time you
find yourself in a situation where you would
normally respond with a negative statement,
you will now automatically say the positive
one. It is as if the old negative has been erased

from your memory banks. In essence, you have created — RE-MINDED — new memories. The process runs something like this: When people come to you with some sad tale of woe, if in the past you said, "POOR BABY" — stop, and examine that thought. You would not want your friend to be poor, so don't program them to be poor. Next time you will be ready with a good expanding expression like "WEALTHY BABY." Try it, it's fun!

Example of your Neggi page.

Date
NEGATIVE STATEMENT

I can't afford that.

POSITIVE REPLACEMENT STATEMENT

I don't wish to buy that now.

Remember each time you cross out the negative poverty statement, you symbolically eliminate it from your vocabulary, from your biocomputer. Have the new positive statement ready in its place. And always... be aware of the words you and others are putting into YOUR computer.

Tune Into Prosperity

As Wallace Wattles says in *The Science of Getting Rich,* "In order to know more, do more, and be more we must have more; we must have things to use, for we learn, and do, and become, only by using things. We must get rich so that we can live more." We must tune into prosperity in order to become all that we can be. For in this day and age, it takes money to live and to learn — to enlarge our potential!

Look to the positive side of prosperity. Use expressions like: "Go first class," "I always have more than I need," "I deserve the best," "I deserve to be wealthy".... Know it is so. Begin to expect and enjoy your prosperous life.

Thinking Wealthy Is Thinking Healthy

Thinking wealthy is part of the balance of life, a part of thinking healthy. Dr. Hans Selye, in his book *Stress Without Distress,* points out the value of thinking in a manner in which you can solve and cope with problems. If you are not at *EASE* with your world, your stressful thoughts will cause *DIS-EASE* within your body.

Science has now proven that stress, or distress as Dr. Selye puts it, is associated with many types of physical, as well as mental and emotional problems. The very words you speak and think are entered into your biocomputer even as you say or think them. It does not matter if these words are in jest, or if you feel that the words have no true meaning. They can become a possible threat to your very life. These are statements that build your personal cage — bar by steel bar. The statements squelch your thinking, and when you try to break out you find your actual survival threatened. The *Mental House Cleaning* process of Steps A and B will help curb the stress as you widen your comfort zone, thus keeping you relaxed on your road to riches.

The True Meaning Of Psychosomatic Illnesss

A psychosomatic illness is not all in your head. "Psycho" means mind, "soma" means body. Psychosomatic is a mind-body related illness. By correcting your speech pattern, your careless statements or speech clutter, you may correct many of your physical problems that you have previously believed too difficult to change.

Many people unnecessarily purchase pills and medicines from their druggist to alleviate psychosomatic illnesses. (Americans take over two tons of aspirin a day!) Some spend enough on headache medicines to bankroll a small business venture in a year. Just think what you could do with that medicine-cabinet money!!

So keep your thinking straight — with thinking wealthy, and thinking healthy.

Sticks And Stones Can Break Your Bones And Words Can REALLY Harm You

What expressions do you use in regard to your health? For example, if you often say: "That job gives me a headache," you will find you get headaches. Do you know someone who repeatedly says, "I wish my boss/wife/husband would get off my back"? It should come as no surprise to find out that individual has back pains. And how many people do you know who say over and over again, "Oh, that's a pain in the... !" Now you know why they sell so much Preparation H (hemmorroid medicine)!!

The words you enter in your biological computer (the brain) will end up reflected in your general health. As James Allen said in *As You Thinketh,* "The bad thought crop will be harvested." So be careful what you say. Being wealthy can be fun only when you are healthy.

Lazy Non-Thinking

Examine closely your present belief structure. Use your Think Wealth Notebook... date your page, and write down all the information you know about money and on becoming wealthy. Now, look at where this information came from and ask, "Is this valid information?" Was it ever valid, or was it a so-called reality handed down from generation to generation? This kind of lazy non-thinking is what keeps the masses, and you, poor. It is lazy thinking which stops us from thinking for ourselves, allows others to do our thinking for us — allows others to even establish our beliefs. We seem to follow that line of least resistance, afraid to change the pattern. Now take a pen and cross out that old "script" — become your own playwright. Write your own future.

Write a new set of beliefs in your Think Wealth Notebook and program them (input them into your brain) with Alphamatics as in "Lesson Ten." Continue to program your biocomputer until you have made all the changes — automatically thinking and saying positives from now on. If you ever find yourself slipping back into negative patterns, say CANCEL, CANCEL! And review your Think Wealth Notebook!

Remember…

"ETERNAL VIGILANCE IS THE PRICE OF SUCCESS."

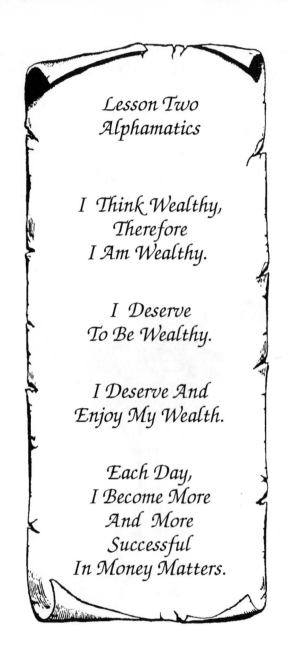

Lesson Two
Alphamatics

I Think Wealthy,
Therefore
I Am Wealthy.

I Deserve
To Be Wealthy.

I Deserve And
Enjoy My Wealth.

Each Day,
I Become More
And More
Successful
In Money Matters.

HOW TO LOOK WEALTHY

Once you are automatically thinking wealthy, your second step will be learning to look wealthy to others — and especially to yourself each time you look in a mirror. The sense of sight controls eighty percent of the sensory information going into and being processed by your biocomputer.

Opinions are formed about you on sight, usually even before you have the opportunity to speak. And, yes indeed, right or wrong, good or bad... first impressions ARE the longest lasting. Many successful people have gone to great lengths just to change a negative first impression. Even the world's finest research has never been able to make a second *first* impression! You will be dealing with successful people who will expect you to be successful as well. And they will judge that by your appearance.

Look wealthy, and you will have the tendency to act and think wealthy. Occasionally someone will suggest that they don't feel comfortable in a suit. You don't always have to wear a suit, but could this be your inner conscious saying, "You are out of your comfort zone"? Is this your inner conscious keeping you in "your place"? You should be comfortable dressed in any manner. And believe me, dressing wealthy is comfortable. It feels good.

I am not saying that you have to dress a certain way to become wealthy, but it is one of the easiest, and fastest ways to change your thinking and behavior patterns. Attire makes the image. Attire can change the thinking and behavior patterns of others toward you!

If you are interested in moving right along, dress the part and it becomes easy to live the part. John T. Molloy in his book *Dress for Success* said:

"Most American men dress for failure. They make four suicidal mistakes: 1. They let their wives or girl friends choose their clothing. 2. They let their favorite salesclerks choose their clothing. 3. They let designer and fashion consultants choose their clothing. 4. They let their background choose their clothing." Molloy's new book, *The New Dress for Success,* is subtitled *The Number One Book to Make You Look Like a Million, So You Can Make A Million.* This book is a must for reading if you are going to climb to the top of the wealth-ladder in the shortest possible time. And, of course, there is also a special edition for women.

Dress Like A Million...
And Even You Will Believe It

Dressing like a millionaire will help both your attitude and your morale, and it does not have to be expensive. Molloy's book will give you the step-by-step plan for a successful wardrobe.

People often comment upon the affluent appearance of my clothes. I no longer tell them where I buy, or how much I pay. It's all part of the money game: getting more value for your money. I never wore cheap suits, but I never paid full price. At least once a month I would go clothes shopping, looking for great buys. Many months would come and go without a purchase, until I found exactly what I wanted at the price I wanted to pay — at one-third the price tag! So be alert for clothing sales, and always comparison shop before you buy.

Today I have all my clothes custom-made in Bangkok, Thailand. Every year or two my wife and I fly to Bangkok and have our clothes made. It's less expensive than buying off the rack — *and* they are custom-tailored! With the money we saved on clothes — we have a "free" vacation!!

The wealthy dress wealthy. They have special clothes for each occasion. Their clothes are clean, well-fitting, never tight, comfortable, and in the best of taste. They can afford it. *So Can You.*

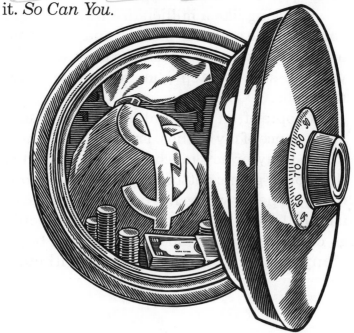

Five Steps To Looking Wealthy

Step One
Hair: Neat, never shaggy; well groomed and well trimmed.

Step Two
Shoes: Always shined, free of scuff marks, and in good repair.

Step Three
Clothes: Of quality material, clean and well pressed.

Step Four
Jewelry: Simple, never flashy.

Step Five
Smile: A smile is the sign of a winner. You are a winner. You are now going to make money. If you see wealthy people who don't smile, they have poverty thinking and are not enjoying their money. Some day a fear will come upon them... they will lose their money, or far worse — their health.

Beware Of The Denture Frown

I once asked a millionaire friend (who otherwise fits every model we discuss in this book) why he never smiled. He said he hadn't noticed but maybe it was because he wore dentures, and it would be very embarrassing if they fell down. Every time I saw him thereafter he was smiling. When I asked him about his bright new smile, he thanked me for bringing the frown to his attention. He said it took quite a bit of practice to develop a natural-looking smile with his teeth closed but it was worth it. He could tell the difference in the way people responded to him. So if your smile is not what it should be, work on it... it's worth it. Whether you wear dentures or not, practice smiling in front of a mirror.

Check Inventory To Your Wealth

Now is a good time for your appearance inventory. *Yes, now, this moment.* Take this book and your Think Wealth Notebook and a pen to any room where you have a large mirror. A floor length mirror is the best. Now, really look at yourself. Make an inventory from head to toe. Be honest, don't kid yourself or make excuses, score yourself as you are now.

Write your score in your notebook for each of the following:

1. Hair: Is your hair appropriately styled for your position in life? (Your new wealthy position, of course.) Rate yourself 1-10; 10 being the best possible hair styling.

2. Dress: Do you dress for your new position in life? Rate yourself 1-10 on your clothing.

3. Appearance: Are you standing straight, in a proud and erect manner? What kind of expression do you have on your face? A wealthy person can enjoy life. Smile. Rate yourself between 1-10 on appearance.

4. Shoes: Rate your shoes. Are they run down at the heels or toes? Are they the right color and style for what you are wearing? Rate yourself 1-10.

5. Impression: If this were the first time you met the person looking back at you from the mirror, would you feel that person was wealthy? Rate yourself 1- 10 on your impression of your wealth.

Now total up your score in your notebook and divide by 5.

#1____ + #2____ + #3____ + #4____ + #5____

= TOTAL ____

TOTAL DIVIDED BY 5= ____ YOUR O.A.R.

This gives your **Overall Appearance Rating.**

Your Success Ship Needs An O.A.R.

Were you honest with yourself on all counts? Good! You NEED to see a prosperous person looking back at you from your mirror. Now you are aware of the areas that need improvement. Are you willing to make the effort to change and improve these most important areas? You are going to make money, so proceed to look wealthy... and you'll find it easier to become wealthy.

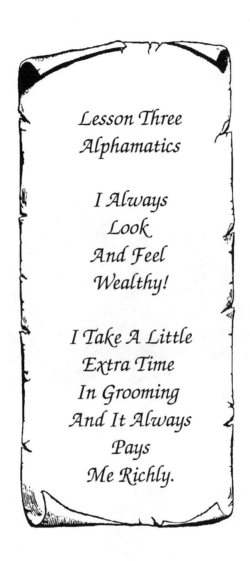

Lesson Three
Alphamatics

I Always
Look
And Feel
Wealthy!

I Take A Little
Extra Time
In Grooming
And It Always
Pays
Me Richly.

HOW TO SPEND WEALTHY

Money is packaged energy — keep it flowing! Money is your personal energy reduced to its most portable form. This energy is unique in that you can send it far away to help in a project that you believe in. And at the same time you can stay at home and do the things that you like best. You might say that money is instant compact energy... all you need is to add love and send it on its way.

Begin thinking of money as energy... and allow this money energy to flow through you. Some people worry about having enough, so they hoard their money.

Aside from stopping the flow, what good is hoarding? You can't enjoy the energy that way. Some say, "I am saving for a rainy day." Really! Even if you could afford to have a "rainy day" would you buy it? Rest assured that if you save for a "rainy day," you will get what you program into your biocomputer — monsoon season!

I spent most of my early life trying to hold on to money..... with little success. My first enlightened moment came after reading one of Catherine Ponder's books, *The Prosperity Secret for the Ages.* This inspired me to pay my bills, even though the amount I owed came to much more money than I had on hand. I paid toward my debts, every cent that I had available, and watched to see what would happen.

My prosperity began to flow almost immediately. The next day I received a large order, by phone, for a product I was manufacturing — and the customer had already mailed his check to pay for the goods in full! That was my start in understanding the *money flow.* Since then, I have always paid my bills promptly, and joyfully. (Well, almost always.)

At one time paying bills caused me stress. Those people wanted my hard-earned money. I didn't understand the flow. There were certain companies that I resented paying, like Mother Bell and General Power. With these companies, I could not shop around. I felt it was a game of *gotcha*. I played all sorts of games like not putting a stamp on the envelope, so they would have to pay the postage when it was delivered. I spent so much energy trying to get even, that I created an even greater resentment. I was going down hill fast...mentally, physically and financially. The breakthrough this time came from Walter Russell, that ultimate genius, written about in a book by Glen Clark, *The Man Who Tapped The Secrets Of The Universe.*

Dr. Russell is quoted as saying, "There should be no distasteful tasks in one's life. If you just hate to do a thing, that hatred for it develops body-destructive toxins and you become fatigued very soon. You must love anything you must do. Do it not only cheerfully, but lovingly and the very best way you know how. That love of the work which you must do anyhow, will vitalize your body and keep you from fatigue."

I found that I hated a lot of things, especially paying bills. In order to break this attitude, I looked for ways to make bill paying fun.

"Who Is This Joy Fully?"

The fun method for paying debts is really quite simple. On each check, on the line where it says "Pay to the order of _____," ignore that phrase, and write, "Joyfully pay to"... and then write the name of the company or person the check is being paid to. This will help you feel better about paying bills. Sound silly? Well it works. Do it on every check you write and you will begin to notice a change in your attitude. And there has never been a problem getting the checks cashed. Some of the fun comes when people cash the checks. One woman, upon presenting the check to the bank teller, was asked, "Who is this Joy Fully"!

Fun With Check Balancing

Balancing your checking account may not be one of your most favorite chores. However, some people write things on checks before they cash them, like "Thank you" or clever sayings. One of my Think Wealth Seminar graduates, a dentist, had a rubber stamp made with a smile face, with the words "Thank You" under the smile face. He stamps each check received front and back with this stamp. This is a great idea. You feel good as you stamp the check, thinking about the other person as they balance their checking account and then discovering the smile face. If you don't have a rubber stamp, you can draw a smile face and write "Thank You" under it. Look for the smile face on any check processed

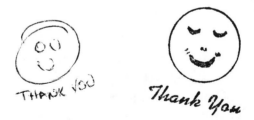

from my office when you receive it back from the bank!

The Seed Money Principle

You can plant a seed and watch it grow. Do this with money, even bill payments. Know that each time you pay out money, you are helping the flow of money, and it will come back multiplied. By paying your debts, you are allowing the money to flow to many salaries and dividends. Each time you are low in funds, give some away. In Jon Speller's book, *Seed Money In Action,* he talks of a man who had only enough money for a roll of pennies, which he proceeded to give away, a penny at a time. When this "came back upon the waters," he moved up to quarters, and gave them away, knowing that each time he gave away money, it would be returned tenfold or more. It worked. *This man is wealthy today.*

A few years ago, I needed to go on a trip to Texas for some special training, and money flow was sluggish at the time. Therefore, I took $10.00 down to the Salvation Army as a donation, knowing it would bring me back $100.00. Thanking me for the donation, the man at the Salvation Army asked if I needed anything from the thrift shop. When I explained that the only thing I needed was luggage, he said that some had just come in. He showed me a beautiful garment bag which looked new, and asked if $5.00 would be too much. Later that day I priced the same bag at a local department store for $175.00!! Ten times, and more! I used that bag for many years, and even bought luggage to match it. Apply this principle yourself, and enjoy the spending.

Play The Money Game

This game uses a small notebook (about 3" by 5") in which you write down everything you spend. Keep track of everything from 25 cents to 25 million dollars. This is great to do for a month each year. You can see exactly where your money goes.

Continue playing the money game by getting more value for your dollar. Divide your expenses into categories: Household (utilities, housing, food); Entertainment; Investing; Travel.... This will give you an idea of exactly where your money flows. See where you can improve on getting more value for your money.

Example: How much money do you spend on food? Explore for restaurants where you can eat *better* for less.

Watch the items you put in your grocery cart. If you buy a better food product, you will enjoy it more, and waste less.

Join a "two for one" club. These clubs are available in many cities. For a fee you will receive a book of coupons or a card entitling you to two meals for the price of one in various fine restaurants around town. Find a friend to share expenses and cut your dining costs in half — while having fun exploring new restaurants and sharing the experience.

Investigate eating better for less. There are many cookbooks on the market, or in the public library, or recipes in the newspaper that employ this theme.

Use your creative imagination, share your ideas with friends who want to live better for less... and they will share theirs with you.

Apply similar ideas to all areas of your expenses... always looking for fun ways to get more value for your money, more "bang for your buck."

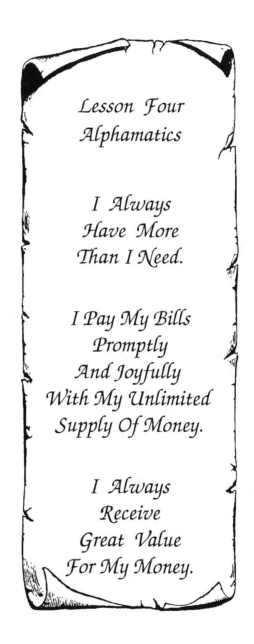

Lesson Four
Alphamatics

I Always
Have More
Than I Need.

I Pay My Bills
Promptly
And Joyfully
With My Unlimited
Supply Of Money.

I Always
Receive
Great Value
For My Money.

HOW TO DECIDE THE PATHWAY TO WEALTH

Many wealth seekers get caught up in the question: How does one know which path to follow on the road to wealth? They become concerned about making the wrong choice, are afraid of choosing the wrong path. Fear and insecurity are the age-old cries of the poverty people. You, as a creative human being, are truly unlimited in your ability to do anything you desire. The path you take to become wealthy is unimportant, although you will want it to be something you enjoy. If you make a less than perfect decision, you can pick yourself up, and start again — with increased experience and know-how.

Babe Ruth, the noted Home Run King, is remembered as holding the record for the most home runs. I wonder how many people know that he also held another record — a record that some would call failure. Babe Ruth also held the record for the greatest number of strike-outs in the history of baseball! The Babe knew that in order to hit the ball you had to swing at it, and that not every swing connects.

Napoleon Hill in *Think and Grow Rich* said, "The majority of people meet with failure because of their lack of persistence in creating new plans to take the place of those which fail." If the first plan you choose does not work successfully, replace it with a new plan. If this new plan fails to work, replace it with still another, and so on until you find a plan which does work. Multimillionaire Mike Todd said, "I have often been broke, but never poor." Remember, "poor" or "poverty" is only a state of mind.

Fear or insecurity keeps poverty eating away at your inner confidence. Do away with fear of failure. Helene Hadsell — called by

Family Circle Magazine, "The lady who wins every contest prize she desires" — wrote in her book, *CONTESTING: The Name It and Claim It Game:* "... there is no failure, only a delay in results." A temporary appearance of failure is all right. Just keep going. You have heard it before, but it's now time to practice the saying, *A quitter never wins and a winner never quits.*

How To Find Your
Personal Success Destination

The first thing to consider is not how you are going to get there, but WHERE YOU ARE GOING. It is amazing how many individuals go through life not knowing where they are going. Most people end up where other people wanted them to go. Their father, mother, husband, wife, girl friend, boy friend, or even their neighbor makes their decisions. Are you living someone else's life, plan, dream? Are you where you are by your choice? Unless you have decided *Your Personal Success Destination,* you will end up at a place that is not truly your life destination. How do we get into such situations? Is it laziness, misfortune, or could the answer be simply the fear of failure? Again, we come back to *comfort zone* — anything beyond a certain income could cause stress or behavior "not like us." So we look for and find excuses to stay within our own cage, our own comfort zone. Most will not take the time to set a Success Destination. It takes effort to plan, effort to change. It seems easier to watch TV: no fear of failure there — just turn the knob, and watch the box... and watch someone else's success...!

The process to discover your Success Destination is simple. All you have to do is to follow a set of rules — the outline given below.

RULE ONE. Decide exactly what you desire and where you want to go — the tangible and the intangible.

RULE TWO. Put these Success Destinations into priority order; that is, which destination automatically leads to the next, and so on... and which destinations are most important to accomplish now?

RULE THREE. Once you know your Destinations, you can then plan how you are going to accomplish or attain them. Don't get caught up in the game of "That's Not It!" Have you ever watched your friends play this game?

They buy a computer, play with it for a while and decide…That's not it!" Next it may be a boat or a new relationship, always ending with "That's not it!" The same pattern is repeated over and over, simply because they never take time to determine what they truly want.

Gold Minding

You can set your mind to discover what you want. The best way to start is by exploring what you really desire. Let's start from scratch. What do you want in your life RIGHT NOW? Examples might be — a finger nail clipper, a new dishwasher, carpeting for your home, new suit, sharp hunting knife, a Mercedes Benz, a college degree, an electric can opener, a larger house, an IBM computer, a hair dryer. Get out your Think Wealth Notebook and draw two lines down the center from top to bottom, forming three columns. Date it then list your *desires.*

Do this now!

Date _FEB 16, 1992_

4-BR HOME	WHITE SHOES	
COMPUTER	SCISSORS	
LASER	SHEARS	
WORLD CRUISE		
CAR		
SOD		

First Things First...
CATEGORIZE — Financial

On another page, draw two lines top to bottom forming three columns, and transfer these same desires — this time divide your list into three categories of *price*. Do this NOW.

Low	Medium	High
WHITE SHOES	LASER	4-BR HOME
SCISSORS	SOD	COMPUTER
SHEARS		CAR
		WORLD CRUISE

Personal Assets

Think about that list. On another page repeat the column process — and make a list of all the assets you will need concerning your attitudes and self-image in order to reach your Destinations. Qualities such as: confidence, creativity, time management, positive disposition, leadership and, of course, good health.

List the *qualities* that you WANT for personal improvement. Do this NOW.

Check for limiting beliefs. Look back on all of your lists. Did you limit yourself? Free yourself of these limits. Free your thoughts, and dream of ANYTHING you desire. Now add a few more items to all of the above.

Your next move is to *prioritize*. Again look at your Success Destinations list, and ask yourself the following questions. Take each Destination separately. Then you will grade or rate your Destination according to — A, B, C, D or E!

A. "Is this Destination *easily obtainable,* within my belief structure?" Consider that can opener, for example. You probably have the money for it now. Is it just a matter of parting with your money? An "A" kind of Destination can be easily obtained with money currently on hand. It is simply a matter of deciding if you really want, or need that object. (These Destinations should take you from one day to one week to obtain.)

B. "Am I ready to put forth the *effort* to attain this Destination? How much do I really desire this item?" A good way to measure desire is to ask yourself, "Am I willing to put forth the necessary extra work to obtain this goal?" Do you want it enough to really work for it? If the desire is strong enough, make this a "B" item. If not, cross it from the your list. (These Destinations should take you from one to six months to achieve... or anywhere from a year to five years.)

C. "Is this *someone else's* Destination, not really MY choice?" Very often in life we wake up to find ourselves fulfilling the dreams of someone else. Remember, it's difficult to be happy if you are living someone else's goal and not your own. If you check any of your items "C," you should decide if you want to keep this Destination. If you don't want it, eliminate it from your list.

D. "Is this Destination in conflict, out of alignment with the other Destinations?" For example, selling boats in the Bahamas may be one Destination, while managing a fur farm in Alaska may be another. It is difficult, if not impossible, going in two directions at once! Line up your Destinations in a plausible order, or eliminate it from your present list. Keep things in their natural sequence.

Fast, successful results will be obtained by looking at the *flow pattern* of all of your Destinations. Your plan will function best when one Destination leads to the next. Like steps... as each Destination is reached, you're already on your way to the next.

E. "Is this plan against the wishes of my family, loved ones, close friends, or boss?" This may be a good time to check your motives. Will this take you a step toward your further happiness and piece of mind? The road will be much easier if you and your family agree on the Destinations.

Example:

can opener (a definite A)

college education (B/C)

this year's model car (A/B)

paint the house (B)

remodel the kitchen (C/D)
get married (C/D/E)
travel the world for 1 year (D/E)
pay off mortgage (B/D)
You get the idea. Now go to it!

At Last — Into Action

This elimination process should have brought your list down to a reasonable size. You should have left only "A's" and "B's" — that which you desire and you can attain. Any C's,D's and E's which are still high personal priority can be moved up to A-B category. Your next step is to copy and sort your list onto another page putting them into five columns of *time frames* — one day.... one week.... one month.... one year.... five years.... or even longer. Generally, items you marked "A" will be done first, items marked "B" will take a bit longer... requiring some additional action. You are now setting a plan of action.

You can turn desires into action by making Success Destination Re-Minder Cards. You have now decided upon the Destinations which are most important to you. The time has arrived to put your *Mind* on your Destinations!

Go out and buy a pack of 3" X 5" filing cards. Get fancy. Go for color! Take three cards and on each write down your major Destinations according to your time frame. These will be your Success Destination *Re-Minder Cards*. These three cards will be identical except on the righthand side you will write vertically on one the words *Car Card, Personal Card* on the second, and on the third *Bedside Card.*

Success Destination Re-Minder Cards

One week   _____

One month _____

Six months _____

One year   _____

Five years _____

Take this book to your local printer — and you can have up to 100 cards reproduced from the next page (for your personal use only) — without need of permission. In excess of 100 copies and copies for others is forbidden by copyright. ALL RIGHTS RESERVED. For your convenience, a six month's supply of 18 Success Destination Re-Minder Cards with positive sayings, may be purchased from the Publisher. For further information and sales

SUCCESS DESTINATION RE-MINDER CARDS

List your goals and set your Destinations for SUCCESS.
Review 15 minutes, three times daily - Every day!

PERSONAL CARD

1 WEEK:

1 MONTH:

6 MONTHS:

1 YEAR:

5 YEARS:

© Dr. Tag Powell 1991, Largo, FL 34643-5117

SUCCESS DESTINATION RE-MINDER CARDS

BEDSIDE CARD

List your goals and set your Destinations for SUCCESS.
Review 15 minutes, three times daily - Every day!

1 WEEK:

1 MONTH:

6 MONTHS:

1 YEAR:

5 YEARS:

© Dr. Tag Powell 1991, Largo, FL 34643-5117

SUCCESS DESTINATION RE-MINDER CARDS

CAR CARD

List your goals and set your Destinations for SUCCESS.
Review 15 minutes, three times daily - Every day!

1 WEEK:

1 MONTH:

6 MONTHS:

1 YEAR:

5 YEARS:

© Dr. Tag Powell 1991, Largo, FL 34643-5117

items, see the supply section in the back of this book.

How To Use Success Destination
Re-Minder Cards

Place one card by your bedside table, one card in your car, and one card in your pocket or purse. Review your Re-Minder Cards frequently, at least three times a day.

The *Bedside Card* is most important — put it by the bed where you can read and mentally picture each Success Destination the last thing at night before going to sleep... and the first thing upon awakening in the morning.

Your *Personal Card* goes in your pocket, wallet or purse. Read and picture your Destinations any time you can... while waiting in the grocery check-out line, in the bathroom, at lunch, and so on.

Place the *Car Card* in your car. Read and image your goals at any opportune time... while waiting for someone, while stopped at traffic lights. Don't worry that you might not know when the light turns green... the person driving the car behind you will notify you a split second after the light changes! Honk, honk!!

When you read your Re-Minder Cards, use the Alphamatics. For years self-help books have stated that you should picture or *visualize* your end results. Practice the following seven steps, and you will find the mystery of visualization easily within your reach. Use these steps when you look at your Re-Minder Cards.

Seven Steps To Improve Visualization

Step One. Pretend to see yourself attaining your Destination. Project your thoughts into the future. Make believe you are really there. Ask yourself, "What would it be like if I were there?" Don't worry about seeing with your eyes — PRETEND you are there... with your mind, with your thoughts.

Step Two. Ask yourself: "Where am I?" What does "there" look like...its shape, its color? Are you in a room, office or outdoors? Imagine the ceiling, the floor, the sky or the ground. What objects do you see in the distance? Now imagine these objects near by. What is the temperature? Are you warm, cold or comfortable? Imagine the sounds of this environment. Do you hear sounds of nature, birds, crickets... or do you hear the sounds of the city, traffic, people talking?

Step Three. Ask yourself, "Who is there?" Think of the people who may be with you at the time you achieve your Destination. Pretend to hear them congratulating you on your success. What would they be saying? Imagine the sounds of their voices — the pitch, the tempo, the words they use. How would you respond?

Step Four. How are you dressed? Think of what you would be wearing. How does the clothing feel on your body? Notice the touch of your shoes, belt, collar, jewelry, eyeglasses, or anything that comes to mind. How would the others be dressed? Start with their shoes and work up. Imagine!

Step Five. What colors are around you? Tune in. What colors would you see in your Destination's environment? Your clothes, other people's clothes? The color of the walls, trees, ocean... anything you can see in your imagined environment!

Step Six. What odors are in the atmosphere around you? What would your Destination smell like? Every place has a certain odor, a special scent. What would it smell like if you were really there? Imagine.

Step Seven. How do you emotionally feel about attaining your success? Are you happy, proud, does it bring tears of joy? Just what is your attitude about this moment? Is it a feeling of satisfaction, of accomplishment? Feel the emotions. Will it make others happy? How would they react? Sense it.

Repeat These Seven Steps Every Time You Think Of Your Destinations... Until You Can Recall Them Easily, Automatically.

Visualization and focused imagination help to program your biocomputer. Many of these areas may be out of your comfort zone. By pretending your results, you expand your mind zone to become more comfortable in these areas. Because your mind has the idea that you have done these goals before, you will have less stress... which in turn will make it easier to make lasting changes and greater movement toward your desires. By seeing yourself at these Success Destinations, you will become more secure in your new way of life. Intentionally directing your thoughts, with purpose, helps overcome many of your self-defeating inner conscious blocks.

YOU WILL BE ABLE TO GET OUT OF YOUR OWN WAY!

The ABC's Of Focusing Power
Using Re-Minder Cards

A. Most importantly, review your Success Destinations during your Alphamatic relaxation time, two or three times daily. And it's a good idea to add your Destinations to your personal audiocassette tape. (See "Lesson Ten")

B. Mark off each Destination as you reach it. It's fun to mark your progress.

C. Take a moment to reflect with *gratitude* on this positive experience.

D. Be sure to write new cards each month. Update your cards each, week or sooner, when you obtain your daily/weekly Destinations!

E. As your one week Destination is met, add another one... and move the month and year Destinations upward as each draws more attainably nearer.

At this point, you have an idea just where you are going. Now, how do you get there? You are learning to focus your thoughts, and have begun to enjoy this "thought power." To get the money to reach your goal, the following is a great tool for focusing in on a specific money amount — perhaps a starting bankroll!

A Magic Tool For Money

Can you imagine someone giving you a check with the money amount left open for you to fill in for any sum you want? That's what I'm about to do — give you a check for unlimited funds. Think carefully before you fill in the amount. This is for real; we are talking about real money.

This magic tool will help your inner conscious mind acknowledge your wealth... and know that you have the amount on the check. This is an easy way to visualize the amount you need because it is something you can physically hold, feel, touch. It is in the form of a check, an item that your mind is accustomed to seeing. This technique has proven effective to a large number of attendees at my THINK WEALTH Seminars. In fact, one businessman wrote that he used this tool to get — hold on to your hat — thirty million dollars! He sent me an eight-page letter describing how he played my audiocassettes, and even taught his staff to use these same principles. Within six months his company had increased their business by thirty million dollars. So use this tool — and start enjoying the results!

What is a check but a contract... or a promise to pay! When you write out a check you mean business. When you fill out your "I Am Unlimited Inc." check (that is now the name of your mental company), you are making a contract with yourself: a promissory note for you to pay yourself the amount written on the check. Your "I Am Unlimited Inc." check is a physical and visual Trigger Mechanism to focus in on your Destination. This is ideal when you need a certain amount of money for a special project.

Pick a specific money amount that you will need for your project. At first it might be a small project, something that will not tax your inner conscious belief. Photocopy the check on the next page. Take a pair of scissors to trim

I Am Unlimited, Inc

69862

92-833
123

Pay to
the order of

_____ 19 ___

$ ___

Bank Of The Universal Mind
4 Uar There Place
Centered, FL 98765-4321

Dollars

For _____

the check to the correct size. (or send a stamped, self-addressed #10 envelope to: FREE CHECK, Top Of The Mountain Publishing, address at the back of this book.) Where it's printed, "Pay to the order of," write in that space "Joyfully pay to… " and put your name. Be sure to write your name in the manner in which you would have someone write out a large sum of money to you. Fill in the dollar amount that you desire on the following space, and write it out in full on the next line.

Now write the reason or what you plan to do or buy with the money on the "For" line. Have something that is easy to visualize. Although a wonderful goal may be to give this amount to help save the whales, it is more effective to write the check for something concrete like a new car. By being concrete and very specific, you increase your Success Ratio of achieving your Destinations.

Before you sign the check, close your eyes and think of yourself in the future; think of yourself getting this amount of money. And pretend to see yourself getting that new car. Become aware that you are making a promise to pay yourself this amount in the future. You are going to make this event happen in some legal, honest manner. Now open your eyes, and joyfully sign the check, aware that this check is now worth the amount you wrote. Carefully place the check with your other money in your purse, pocket or wallet. Each time you pay out any money, take a moment to look at this check drawn on your unlimited funds from the *Bank of the Universal Mind.* Think of your Success Destination — receiving this amount of money. And yes, expect the check to be cashed!

Stay alert for opportunities for this money to come to you. You may receive it in one lump sum, or you may receive various amounts which total the full amount. In the book, *Illusions,* by "wealthy" Richard Bach, he says, "We are never given a wish without the power to make it so. We may have to work for it however." The secret is knowing that you will get this money, that you will work honestly and justly to obtain it. It will be so.

When the amount written on the check has materialized, write and tell us of your success, and send us the old check with a stamped, self-addressed envelope. We will send you a new check to fill out for a new project. We keep a file of the checks sent in, as well as the success stories. We have so many now, maybe we will write a book with just the success stories of the checks. Keep working your way up, step by step... or check by check.

One couple, Marty and Ron Folmer, are on their third or fourth check the last time I looked. Their Success Destination list had twenty-two items. With the second check returned, Marty and Ron's letter said that they had reached twenty-one of their Destinations. Number sixteen on their list was to get their carpet cleaned. They did not get this one — they got a new house instead! Their new home is a $175,000 lakefront dream house with a pool. Oh yes, the Mercedes they programmed for looks great in the driveway. When you apply the techniques, THEY WORK... just ask the Folmers.

Mail in your accomplished Destination check and your success story with a stamped, self-addressed #10 envelope to: Top Of The Mountain Publishing, 11701 South Belcher Road, Suite 123, Largo, Florida 34643-5117 USA.

Lesson Five
Alphamatics

Wealth
Is Mine
Now
That I Have
Set My Success
Destinations.

I Enjoy
My Life
And My Wealth,
For
My Funds
Are Unlimited.

I Have Unlimited
Funds
In My Universal
Bank Account.

HOW TO GET WEALTHY

You have discovered where you are going — your Destinations. Now it is time to find the vehicle in which to get there. How do you get wealthy? The answer is: The methods are endless. Money is everywhere, and is just waiting to be used, to be directed.

Ten Moves To A Million Dollars

Want a quick easy plan to make a million dollars? Just think of a way to double your money ten times! Let's use $1,000.00 to start. First find a way to double that one thousand to two thousand. "Not too hard," you say. Next, go from two thousand to four thousand; from four thousand to eight thousand; eight thousand to sixteen thousand; sixteen thousand to thirty-two thousand; thirty-two thousand to sixty-four thousand; sixty-four thousand to one hundred twenty-eight thousand... to two hundred fifty-six thousand... to five hundred twelve thousand... to one million, twenty-four thousand!

Yes, there can be just ten steps to a million dollars. Or you can find something that sells for $2,000.00 but costs you $1,000.00 — and just sell a thousand of them. This may be an over simplification, but remember, it's only as hard as you believe it to be.

An excellent source for some ideas is in your public library. Ask your librarian where to look for books on money-making ideas. Books by Charles Givens' have been successful in helping many people.

The Stock Market

All wealthy people own stock, bonds, CDs, money market accounts, gold or silver certificates. So, your next step is to buy some stock... right now. While you are thinking wealthy, you can be getting wealthy. There is a special feeling about owning stock. So if you do not own any get started now toward your wealthy image.

You Can Own Stock Right Now

A few years ago, I bought some stock. I diversified — stock in an airline, electronics, oil, and a computer manufacturer. (An interesting note is that all have folded into the night except the computer stock.) While talking to my broker at that time, I discovered a little known fact for the beginning financier: Most stock brokers will sell you as little as $5.00 worth of stock, and you can receive a stock certificate which looks great! The broker won't be thrilled with the sale, and there is usually a brokerage charge of under $15.00 on the $5.00 transaction. But for a total of about $20.00 you can become a stock owner! So, if you don't already own stock, purchase some and join the wealthy.

Create A Money Power Wedge

Buy $25.00 of stock from your broker each week, and in a year you will have $1,300.00 in stocks, plus the profit (if any) from your investment. In most cases it is better than putting money in a bank, as long as you stay in the main stream investments. Stock goes up and down so be sure to invest only what you can afford to lose. As soon as you have invested a bit of money, you will have a wedge for the power moves for increasing your wealth.

Choosing A Broker

I asked my friend, retired stock broker, Jim Brunner, about choosing a broker. Here are his thoughts:

"When first contacting a broker you might want to call ahead and ask for a broker with some years with the firm. Whether you walk into a brokerage office or contact one by phone, you will usually be referred to the floor broker of the day, unless a friend or acquaintance has referred you to someone specific. You should make it a point to sit down with the broker and go over your special requirements. This will help him to know how to handle your account properly. Opening an account with a broker is very similar to opening one with a bank, although the paperwork may be somewhat different." Also consider mutual funds. These are listed, rated in various business or money magazines. By all means, do read these.

In the meantime... especially in a slow economy... *keep your cash and credit "dry."* When the market is down — that is the time to buy. But if your credit and cash are over-extended, you won't be able to take advantage of a down market. So spend and invest wisely. If you get to be a real "pro" and think you know your stocks, then consider a discount broker. But be careful. The market is too volatile for anyone with low "risk tolerance"!

Beware Of The Credit Card Trap

It is true you have unlimited funds, but be aware that obtaining a loan or using a credit card is drawing on someone else's money. The old cliche "Never a Borrower or Lender Be" is good advise in most cases. Create your wealth using *your own money* for if you lose it, the only one you have to answer to is yourself... and you can always generate more money. When you borrow or use a credit card you are involving a second party who MUST get paid with interest. This fact alone could put you out of operation. If things get hard when using your own money, you can always tighten your belt and continue to function. As far as lending money is concerned — it can put you in the position of a bill collector. No one likes to be a bill collector — and often there is nothing left to collect. The number one rule is: *never loan money you can't afford to loose.*

There Is Only So Much Land

Probably the best and safest way to increase your financial portfolio is by investing in Real Estate. One of the few commodities that cannot be manufactured to supply and demand is land. The demand and price of any real estate, given enough time, will always spiral upward. Of course, there are always exceptions to the rules.

Real estate has probably made more millionaires than any other field of endeavor. Trainer and financial expert Robert Allen has two books on getting wealthy in real estate, and his new book, *No Money Down for the 90's* is also a good reference. Overall, real estate is probably the safest investment in the long run. But again, try to buy in a down market — and if the economy is weak, be sure you are financially able to "wait" for that upswing in real estate — for it always comes.

How To Assure Every Investment You Make Will Be Successful

You may loose your money in any investment. This is the chance you take when you play the money game. You can turn failure into success if you learn something from every loss or gain. Most people go through life continuously repeating the same mistakes. I have a friend who at last count has been miserably married four times, to four different women, the last three being a carbon copy of his first wife. The only real difference is that one was thin, one was heavy, one was tall, and one was short. To date, he has not learned. Turn each mistake, each loss into a valuable learning experience. Be careful never to repeat the same mistake twice... then every investment you make *will* be successful at some level.

The next section is to give some creative ideas of departure to widen your scope of thinking. These will help your mind to spring board you to success, and to stimulate your creative mind.

Invest In Yourself...
Put Your Money Where YOUR Mind Is!

You are your greatest investment and your greatest resource. Invest time and money in yourself. A study conducted by the American Express Company showed investment in *personal training* reaped the greatest return for the money. The study showed that over a ten year span, the personal training investment was multiplied many times over in increased earnings... many times more than real estate, stocks or bonds. In fact, more than any other type of investment!

So take courses and seminars for self-improvement. If your funds are still a bit limited, buy books or go the public library... and read! There are many fine home study courses available. Take courses through TV college and university programs. View them even if you don't register for college credits. In most areas there are special TV channels for study-at-home courses. If you are at work while these shows are on the air, invest in a VCR, and video-record the shows for later viewing.

A word about high school and college: if you are currently in school — finish! Get your diploma! The most *important* lessons learned are in most cases subjective — training in discipline, perseverance, successful social interaction skills... and self-confidence! These are worth their weight in gold, and will help bring you "gold" in later life.

Ten Steps To Tap Into Your Creativity

STEP ONE: What do you like to do? Get out your Think Wealth Notebook, and make a list of all things you enjoy doing or things that you do well. Write down everything — the silly things, the fun things, the things you find interesting. Look at this list for a source of becoming wealthy. People will always pay for something that others do well. Why not do what you enjoy? Review your list and think of how you can make money. Stay loose with your thinking. Write down ALL of your ideas, even if they seem crazy and improbable. Often some of my best ideas are lost simply because I didn't write them down.

One of my seminar graduates found that she enjoyed baking. In fact, her friends told her that she made the best cheesecake in the world. After taking my seminar, and going through this process of tapping into her creativity, she opened the *"Classic Cheesecake Company."* After creating and testing about sixty different flavors of cheesecakes, she started a Cheesecake-of-the-Month Club. The customer had a choice: the flavor of the month or one of their old favorites. Her next move was to contact restaurants in the area to supply them with her cheesecakes... offering a different flavor each week.

She had cardboard table tents printed to place on each table, promoting the flavor of the week. The last time I talked to her she was looking to franchise Classic Cheesecake Mini-

Concessions in the shopping malls. This is an example of trusting in your own creative abilities.

STEP TWO: Tap into the creativity of others. Be creative in your thoughts of helping others. Look for their special and unusual abilities, and help bring these forth. You can market their products, their special talents.

Look for "piggyback" ideas that can ride upon the success of another. A good example of this is the Teenage Mutant Ninja Turtles. Millions have been made by marketing "sideline items" (products that display and promote the name of a well-known commodity), such as tee-shirts, games, toys, posters. The manufacturer of these items pays a royalty to the copyright owner. Stay tuned to what's happening. Take *quick* ACTION and you will reap the rewards.

STEP THREE: Keep your mind open to what is new...then look a step further. To what other ideas does this new product or idea lead? What are the future results of its use? And what future needs will be created?

A hot idea comes from the continuing microcomputer boom. Almost every business has a computer... as well as many homes. Millions of microcomputers have been sold. The challenge today are two-fold: *1.* How to use the computer, and *2.* Finding competent computer repair people. Most "users" today are not computer buffs, they simply want to get the most out of their computer — to get the machine to perform just like the computer store told them it would. You might learn how to use the most popular software, and then learn how to train others to use these programs. (Most programs have tutor disks available on which to base your training.)

Or you might go into computer repair. No, it is not that difficult. And those that really know their business are booked months in advance. One repairman, whom I consider to be less than the best, is quoting $100.00 per hour. There are several good learn-at-home courses on computer repair.

STEP FOUR: Stay tuned in to opportunity. Very often that great idea passes by unnoticed. Stay alert! How about doing THINK WEALTH workshops? All across the country, people are conducting these workshops by purchasing multiple copies and using this book as a workbook. You can use it page by page as your textbook. You will be helping this planet eliminate poverty, while at the same time making money for yourself. Write the Publisher for special workshop volume discounts.

Opportunity abounds with fax machines — soon every business will have one, and it won't be long before the fax invades the home. What new ideas can you think of regarding marketing with a fax? One good idea would be for a sandwich shop to allow business people to fax their lunch orders. Restaurant fax machines could each day send lunch menus and daily specials to local businesses and offices. The home marketing of these machines is now opening up. Figure out uses and ideas for the fax in the home, and quickly market your idea — before the rest of the fax-world beats you to it!

STEP FIVE: Keep your thinking unlimited. They laughed at the Wright Brothers, Fulton, Ford, and at the possibility that one day people would walk on the moon. Each of these pioneers opened a new world for jobs and opportunities. What ideas do you have lurking in your mind? Your ideas may be impossible, silly or funny. Write them down, look at them later. You might find a gold mine.

It seems like only yesterday when I was sitting in the V.I.P. section at Cape Kennedy Space Center waiting for the very first launch of the space shuttle COLUMBIA. I was reflecting on how exciting it was to be living in this space age where the mind is producing such great marvels. (By the way, many millions of dollars have been made from "spinoffs" of the space program — eyeglass cleaners, dishes, pacemakers and many more.) If you go to Russia, you can now buy space on a future space shuttle. Can you think of a way to market "space" to others? What are some of the needs that you can think of for the future?

STEP SIX: Look for the NEEDS of others. A graduate of my Seminar thought to supply a need by examining one of the greatest problems of the day: chemical waste that is being dumped into our environment. Upon further study she found that certain waste products could be reused in the fabrication of other chemicals. Today she makes a good living finding a waste product from one company which will supply a need for another company.

Look to recycling. Many items besides chemicals can be a waste product for one company and a reusable treasure for another. Packing material is a good example — look for a company that receives a product with a large amount of packaging, look for another company to buy this waste material to repackage their own items. And the original company may even pay you to haul the waste away!

Fulfill the needs of others by writing it down! Write a book on a subject with which you are familiar, or choose a topic from your "enjoy doing" list. Other people may gain benefit from your knowledge. Supply a need — fill the information gap in your expert field.

One author wrote a book helping microcomputer owners to make a profit working at home. The book is selling very well, and he even had offers for the purchase of translation rights from foreign countries.

Another author wrote a book on making home movies with your VCR camera. He has written several books, each one containing different scripts for plays that you and your friends can act at home and record on your VCR. Remember, look for a need (entertainment) and supply that need (the viewer becoming involved).

If you have an idea for a book, write an outline and first chapter, and submit it to our Publisher: Top Of The Mountain Publishing, 11701 S. Belcher Rd., #123, Largo, Florida 34643-5117 USA. Who knows, you may have a bestseller!

STEP SEVEN: Look toward services. The promise of opening your own business is greater than ever before. Many of the old service providers are gone, and have left the field wide open for a smart operator. When is the last time you had your shoes resoled? See what I mean? So look not only to providing a new service, but bringing back an old and needed one. What service would you like to use? So start it!

Do you like to travel? See the world and get paid for it! We just discovered how to open a travel agency at home for less than $2000 — complete with training, computer program and hook up for booking airlines. You can enjoy helping people go on vacation by land, sea or air, and enjoy traveling yourself for little cost. Travel agents can currently fly round trip from the U.S. to London\Paris for $150; anywhere in the world round trip for $300! Or cruise on the finest cruise lines, in the best available cabin, for $35 per day. Sounds like a fun career, doesn't it? If you are interested, drop me a line care of the publisher, and I will see that a reliable company I know of sends you information on how to become a travel agent at home.

STEP EIGHT: Always do MORE than you are paid for. A must for fast success. This is one of the greatest secrets in becoming wealthy. If you are one who says that you give a dollar's work for a dollar's pay, you will spend your whole life as a wage slave. Whether it's a service or a product, always give a little bit more.

STEP NINE: Help others become more successful, and they will help you. This principle has built Amway, American Horizons, Mary Kay and of course, Avon. These are all giant industries that deal with helping others help others make money. *The Wall Street Journal* reported that by the year 2000, a major percent of all goods will be sold by network marketing. Last year, out of the five top companies creating the most millionaires, four were multi-level (network marketing) companies. These success stories are true, but they take a lot of work and time.

If you are looking toward multi-level marketing be sure to go with a good company which has a complete training program. If you have the confidence and time you might want to first go with a top company, learn the principles, and then start your own company. Many of those in existence today were started by people who spun-off from other companies. Today most network/multi-level companies are 100% legal and are not the old pyramid-type marketing.

STEP TEN: What are you waiting for — do it NOW! Don't put anything off due to "I don't have enough money"... "I don't know enough"... "It hasn't been done yet." When you have an idea, follow through with it — and reap the rewards!

It's not too surprising if you never heard of Elisha Gray or The Gray System. Elisha was a very innovative person. He had ideas, but it seems that he spent more time talking about his ideas than putting them into action. That seemed not to matter because when he got going he could accomplish much in a very short period of time. He had an idea, a good idea, and many called it a great idea. He finally got around to putting his idea on paper, and he created a working model. On the way to the patent office, he stopped at a friend's house for lunch and to show off his idea. He reached the patent office a short time later. But it seems that two hours before, another person had filed a patent for almost the same idea. Mr. Gray was two hours too late for you to ever hear of or use the Gray System. Of course you know of the Bell System — named for Alexander Graham Bell, the young man who had arrived two hours earlier. The patent was for the telephone. And in case there is any doubt in your mind — this is a true story. Whenever you feel like procrastinating, think of Mr Gray. That should jump start you into action. DO IT NOW!

There is no greater time in our history for you to become wealthy than right now. Do it!!!

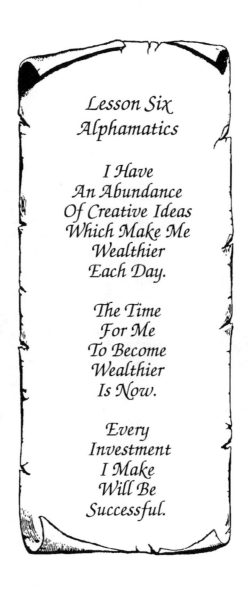

Lesson Six
Alphamatics

I Have
An Abundance
Of Creative Ideas
Which Make Me
Wealthier
Each Day.

The Time
For Me
To Become
Wealthier
Is Now.

Every
Investment
I Make
Will Be
Successful.

106

HOW TO PLAN YOUR
MONEY MOVES

There is a multitude of books telling you how to invest, and where to put your money so that it will grow. I leave these details to them. However, here are some important points for starters:

Invest your money — don't *save* it. After all, what are you saving it from? A fate worse than death? What's the difference between "saving" and "banking" money? Attitude! A poor person "saves" money. A wealthy person "banks" money.

How To Choose A Bank

Shop for a bank as any customer would shop for a service. When you shop for a washing machine, you know that all washing machines wash clothes. However, some machines will fit your washing needs better than others. So too will some banks fit your money needs better than others. Become accustomed to their "hallowed" halls.

Wear a good suit and tie (dress or scarf), go to *several* different banks — and ask to speak to the President. Tell them you are thinking of opening a business account, you are interested in finding out about their bank, and you would like to meet the President. You probably will not meet the bank President, but who knows, you might, and if you do I sure would bank there. Whoever you speak with, ask them about the bank, noting what services they offer. This is fun and also makes you feel comfortable in the bank environment.

Most people are not comfortable in banks. Note the hushed tones in which people speak. Are you overly impressed? Ever notice that you-are-not-in-charge feeling when you are in the area of the loan officer? Columbia University conducted several weeks of research, studying the behavioral patterns of people in New York banks. Generally, they found that when a person enters a bank they becomes extremely tense and alert. There seems to be a major difference when you compare people entering a bank as opposed to entering other types of businesses.

Realize that a bank is nothing but a *money store,* just like any other store. You can shop around, and in some cases you might choose to use several, each for a different purpose. Allow yourself to be comfortable in all areas of a bank. If in the future you desire to "rent some money," you can walk in with confidence. Banks are in business to rent money. (The poor say, "to loan money.") You will want to rent money for the least cost, and it will always help if you know the President or Vice-President of the bank you choose for your needs. And it sure will make you more comfortable!

We know that wealthy people have more than one bank account. Why not you? Let's have you open three — yes, I said THREE — different accounts. To make it more fun, and to become comfortable in banks and banking procedures, try three different banks!

Start your Growth Money Investments. Each week you will put all of your money into just one account, your *Working Income Account,* then you will transfer monies to separate channels most profitable to you. The amount you put into each account each week is not important. The important thing is: *You are taking action to change your thinking about money.*

1. My WORKING INCOME
Checking Account Goal — To build your financial responsibility. To discipline your money matters.

Technique — Every cent you earn goes into this account. From this one, you write checks to pay your bills and then to transfer funds to your other accounts. Note: No matter how small an amount, always leave some money of each deposit IN this account.

2. My INVESTMENT INCOME
Savings Account

Goal — To have the money people say you have to have to make money... "It takes money to make money."

Technique — You take money out of this second account only when you are going to make more money with it (through investments, starting a business). Then all that money you make goes back into this account. What you are attempting to do is double your money each year. Remember... if you start with $1,000, at the end of ten years, you will have over a million dollars! Even if you take nothing out, you should still put enough money in to see that it is doubled each year.

Tip — Most banks have "interest on checking" (a special savings account you can write checks on). Why not have your money earn interest while its sitting in your account? Let your money work for you... every minute of the day, even while you sleep!

3. My FUN AND GAMES ACCOUNT
Savings Account

Goal — To have money to do things when you want, just for the fun of it, and to develop a habit of spending for fun. Enjoy spending for the BIG things (eliminate compulsive spending on the very many little things).

Technique — You must spend the balance in this third account (except for $10) every three months. Four times a year you will *enjoy* the money in this account, but be sure to continue putting money into it. You may use this money for the BIG things you desire. Remember the Eleventh Commandment, *"Thou shalt have thy jollies."* Enjoy...and make a habit of it.

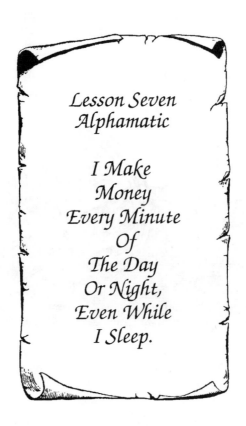

Lesson Seven
Alphamatic

I Make
Money
Every Minute
Of
The Day
Or Night,
Even While
I Sleep.

HOW TO BECOME
ACCUSTOMED TO WEALTH

Do you think it would be easy to become accustomed to wealth? For some, believe it or not, it is actually hard work. They spend so much of their time worrying about losing their money, they soon lose their enjoyment in *using* their money. So you can start now to enjoy your wealth!

Renowned author/lecturer Dr. Leo Buscaglia once told me an exercise he presented to his students. He asked them to write what they would do if they had only three days to live. When he graded the papers he would mark on each, "What are you waiting for? Do it

NOW!" You want to be a millionaire? Live like a millionaire NOW! Use your Alphamatics and pretend you are wealthy. See yourself doing the things a millionaire would do.

How To Live Wealthy

Knowing that you will be a millionaire in say, a year from now, what would you change in your life TODAY? For example, in the first four months of this year: I purchased a new car — a new Le Baron convertible; I sailed on a cruise; I flew to the Orient and had my clothes tailor-made; and this month my wife, Judi, and I are off to London.

Now, you do something BIG that you've been wanting to do, but putting it off until "tomorrow."

Always Keep Some "Fun Money"
In Your Pocket

At your earliest opportunity, put two five dollar bills into the hidden compartment of your wallet. Now you know that you never will be without spending money. As soon as you are feeling more prosperous, change this amount to two $10's. When you are comfortable with that amount, change the bills to $20's, and so on until you always have two one-hundred dollar bills in your wallet. This enhances your continued feeling of prosperity.

While reading this, I had not checked my stash for a while. I looked into my hidden compartment and "found" five $100 bills! That's "Fun Money."

An interesting note: I rarely need to spend this "Fun Money," but I always know it's there if I need it. This stops a lot of false wishful thinking, like "If I had the money I would buy that." Because I have the "stash" I know I have the money and I don't really need or even really desire "that item."

Start NOW To Live Wealthy!

- ☐ Start going to the better restaurants. They cost only a few dollars more per person than cheaper places. You will find the food, service, atmosphere and your overall feeling to be much better.
- ☐ See a play in the best seats available in the house.
- ☐ Take a trip. Go away for the weekend. Take a suite, not a room.

- ❏ Buy a good audiocassette player/recorder. (I recommend a Superscope by Marantz.)
- ❏ Go to a hair stylist or hair dresser, and get the works.
- ❏ Do what you want for one day. Stay in bed, play golf, go swimming, read a book, watch TV, even eat junk food.
- ❏ Buy a set of matched luggage.
- ❏ Call a distant friend or relative you haven't seen in awhile; have a nice long chat.
- ❏ Buy a really good car, a new one if you like. Buy one you have always wanted to own.
- ❏ Call the office to say you just won't be in today. (Note: DO NOT say you are sick.)
- ❏ Call your stock broker and buy some stock.
- ❏ Call your real estate broker to look at income property (even if you are not planning to buy).
- ❏ Buy season tickets for your local theater or sports team franchise.
- ❏ Buy a new suit or outfit, complete with accessories.

❏ Get out your Think Wealth Notebook and list other things that YOU can think of... that will change and build your money confidence.

❏ Now, DO some of them with your new money attitude!

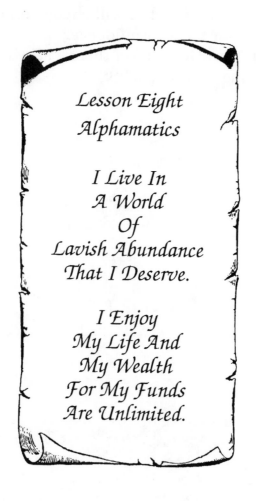

Lesson Eight
Alphamatics

I Live In
A World
Of
Lavish Abundance
That I Deserve.

I Enjoy
My Life And
My Wealth
For My Funds
Are Unlimited.

HOW TO DEVELOP
MONEY CONFIDENCE

Developing money confidence is a step-by-step procedure. If you say, "I wish I had a million dollars!" you need to know how much is a million dollars. You can not obtain what you can not imagine.

Accept your MIND as a cornucopia of wealth. The only shortage is the lack you create. As soon as you accept that there is enough money for everyone to enjoy the *abundance-reality* you are creating in your waking and sleeping dreams... you open your world to the natural flow. One of the greatest books ever written on money thinking is *The Science of*

Getting Rich by Wallace Wattles. He points out that you can't help the poor by giving them money or food. Only by helping them learn to properly THINK, will they break their chains of poverty. Anything else is a waste of your energy and theirs... leading only to false hope.

It was on the way home from a fishing trip with my father when he turned to me and said, "Well son, now you will never go hungry." When I asked him why, my Dad replied, "Your grandfather always told me that 'If you give a person a fish he will eat for one meal; if you teach a person to fish he will eat for a lifetime.' You now know how to fish!"

Our welfare system gives the poor a meal; what they really need to learn is how to fish for money and success. If you want to help people, don't give them money — give them a copy of my book or the Wattles' book... or both. You stand even a better chance of having them read and use the techniques if you sell them these books — remember one of our earliest programs: Nothing is for free... you have to pay for the good things in life. By all means, be sure that your children read these books... and then discuss the ideas with them. Teach them to fish!

You are not in competition with anyone, including yourself. Your success, if you apply these principles correctly, will not be at the expense of someone else. There is abundance… more than enough for everyone… to make the effort to become free of negative poverty thinking.

Consider the thought, "I will do better today than I did yesterday." This presupposes that you did not do your best yesterday. Each day, each minute is different, and the winners make the most of each minute, each day. Do your best *now*, not because you are trying to outperform yourself, but because the joy of life is in doing the very best with your ability at this and every minute coming next. Remember life is the continuous unfolding of a beautiful and fascinating adventure. If you are not getting that, you are doing it wrong!

Can The Can'ts

You can do anything that anyone else can. In fact, it is easier if you watch others and read about others and find out how they did it… then duplicate it… and even improve on it! If you free yourself from the "I can't" limitations you will be doing things you have never done before... and just possibly have never been done before! Get off the beaten path and blaze a trail for others to follow!

The Three Basic Laws Of
Successful Programming

The three basic laws of successful mental programming are: Desire, Belief, and Expectancy. When all three of these are activated, the Success Formula will work.

Law One: *DESIRE,* not want. Are you willing to do all that is legally and honestly possible to earn that million dollars? Do you truly desire to be wealthy? As a Master said, "The one who moves mountains, goes toward the mountain with a goal in mind and a shovel in hand, knowing that mountain WILL move — ONE WAY or ANOTHER!"

Law Two: *BELIEF.* If the wealth you are programming for is beyond your imaging power, your inner belief will not be adequate. The true limiting factor is YOUR imagination.

If your friend is programming for a million-dollar bank account when his average balance is $100, your friend probably will not be successful because it is beyond his imagining power. You might recommend to your friend that his first step be to mentally program for a $1,000 bank balance (which is within his belief structure). He should attain that step first, in order to know how it feels, and then on to build an image of how $10,000 will feel!

After programming for $10,000 and attaining it, your friend can now build an image of $100,000, and so on, always building toward the EXPECTANCY of the million dollars — and building a strong BELIEF along the way.

The game of golf gives us a good example of a Negative Belief: When some golfers see a water hazard between them and the green, they will often pick up the new ball they are playing and replace it with an old cheap "practice" ball. They don't want to lose their good expensive ball in the water trap! And even when the water hazard is small, with much good turf surrounding it... the ball will usually end up in the water. Why? Because their belief that the water hazard was a hazard insurmountable— led to their negative action... the switching of the golf balls — the mind (thought) sent a message to the brain which caused the body to swing the golf club to hit the ball into the water!

Law Three: *EXPECTANCY.* Watch a good golfer when he swings. Notice the perfect arc of the club after the ball is hit, and how the swing is totally completed before the pro looks to see where the ball went. Now notice the poor golfer... he tries to see where the ball went as soon as he hits it, thereby cutting his swing. The poor golfer is afraid... afraid he will lose the ball to the woods, sand traps, water hazards. The poor golfer has the desire, and sometimes even the belief, that he can hit the ball correctly... the pro *expects to hit it correctly.* We might call *Expectancy the action "follow-through" of Belief.*

Magic Imagination Exercise

A good exercise for your imagination will be to spend a short time daily imagining what it will be like one year from today, when you will be a millionaire (or whatever financial goal you have in mind). For right now you may find it more believable to imagine $5,000 — and then work toward imagining $50,000. Set the figure to suit your present BELIEF STRUCTURE.

Plan what you will do with the money when you have it. Plan it in all detail — and put it in writing!

Consider how this will affect what you are doing today. How will receiving this money affect what you will be doing for the next twelve months? You don't have the money yet, but the best time to PREPARE for this windfall is NOW.

Begin to adjust your life and your NOW. Keep your ATTITUDES and your life flowing toward your wealth at a nice smooth pace. Enjoy confidence today, and look forward to your wealthy future tomorrow.

The True Secret Of Money Confidence

The true secret of money confidence is *confidence in yourself.*

The development of knowledge of yourself will open the door to a new world of SELF-WORTH. Of the numerous seminars and courses given to increase self-confidence, they all work on the exterior you. Self-worth is the *inner you.* To develop this confidence, you need to know the real you, the *now you.*

An inventory of your qualities will prove vastly effective. Taking inventory is the most important part of any business. You must know what you have on hand in order to know what you need.

I am reminded of one of the world's most famous success stories, the building of the McDonald's fast food empire: Ray Kroc at age 52 approached the McDonald brothers to do promotion for their hamburger stand. When Ray Kroc first started promoting the McDonald Brothers' Hamburgers he spoke of the McDonald Brothers as becoming a billion dollar business. The brothers could not believe in Kroc's projected future. Their attitude was, "If you think it's so good, why don't you do it?"... so Ray Kroc bought the business! The rest is history. (Many successful merchandising ideas today come from a special *meditation room* with very comfortable chairs at the McDonald's Headquarters.)

Successful Inventory Idea

Part of the genius of the operation is that every McDonald's restaurant knows where it stands at the end of each shift. The inventory system at McDonald's is a brilliant idea. They do not count hamburgers, pounds of coffee, or gallons of soda. They count containers... hamburger containers, coffee cups, soda cups, etc. By subtracting this number from the amount counted at the end of the previous shift, they know how much has been sold. They know too, what they have on hand, and what should be ordered. This may be the reason you never see a McDonald's go out of business — they know where they stand.

It is a wise idea to know where one stands. Apply this inventory policy to you and your life. Is it hard to tell where you are in life by asking yourself about you? Try counting your containers. For now, let's count your emotional "containers," your feelings about things. For how you feel can have a deciding effect on how far you go. (Are your containers half full or half empty?)

The Personal Inventory

A personal inventory can be taken in a very short time and will be most rewarding. Watch your confidence soar from knowing just where you are, how far you have grown. Get out your Think Wealth Notebook and begin by listing your emotional assets and liabilities such as the following.

Rate yourself on a scale of 0 to 10; a very low rating is 0, and 10, of course, is the top rating. Think about each area, rate yourself... and then write an example.

CONFIDENCE   ASSET _____5_____

Example:

I have very little difficulty when meeting new people. I introduced myself to John Doe last week, and enjoyed the encounter.

INSECURITY   LIABILITY _____7___

Example:

I feel insecure with very successful people. I avoided calling the supervisor about a very important meeting I was supposed to attend.

When you finish the following personal inventory, total your assets, and your liabilities. This is a picture of what you think of you. You will work toward *the sum of your assets being greater than the sum of your liabilities.*

Copy the following suggested evaluation ideas
to your Think Wealth Notebook and take this
simple inventory of yourself NOW.

CONFIDENCE   ASSET _____
Example _____

INSECURITY   LIABILITY _____
Example _____

HONESTY   ASSET _____
Example _____

DISHONESTY   LIABILITY _____
Example _____

GIVING   ASSET _____
Example _____

GREEDY   LIABILITY _____
Example _____

PATIENCE   ASSET _____
Example _____

IMPATIENCE   LIABILITY _____
Example _____

LOVING   ASSET _____
Example _____

HATRED   LIABILITY _____
Example _____

TOLERANCE   ASSET _____
Example _____

PREJUDICE   LIABILITY _____
Example _____

DOING IT TODAY   ASSET _____
Example _____

PROCRASTINATION   LIABILITY _____
Example _____

OTHERS _____

   TOTAL ASSETS _____

   TOTAL LIABILITIES _____

Serve Your Assets On A Silver Platter

Work toward the sum of your assets always being greater than the sum of your liabilities.

Review the liabilities to see what you need to work on to improve your self-worth. A very effective and easy system is to put each liability on a separate small slip of paper, fold each one a few times, and put them in a small tray atop your dresser. Each day, before leaving, draw one slip... and enjoy the day turning that liability into an asset.

For example, if your liability is *procrastination,* especially for that day, look for ways to do things *now...* not putting off even the smallest thing that needs to be done today. *Tip:* make sure you do not fall into the trap of doing tomorrow's easy work today. Don't put off doing the harder work. Turn procrastination into *perseverance.* Do this each day — take a different liability and turn it! Do this and you will know that every day you are improving your self-worth, both mentally and financially.

Lesson Nine
Alphamatics

Every Day I Am
Improving My
Self-Worth,
Both Mentally
and Financially.

It Is Okay
For Me To Have
Everything I Desire.

Every Day
I Have
Increasing
Confidence In My
Money Dealings

HOW TO REACH THE ALPHAMATIC PROGRAMMING LEVEL

This final lesson is designed to guide you in reaching your Alphamatic programming level. These mental training exercises will help you attain and function at the *Alpha brainwave frequency* (inner conscious mind). Alpha is associated with stronger programming of information, increased creativity, improved memory, and general well-being. Many top psychologists agree that Alphamatic programming will produce faster results.

Alphamatic programming is believed to bypass the normal "left brain" *analytical* function, and directly involve the *creative* functioning of the "right brain." This saves hours, days, or months in correcting any negative programming.

You can reprogram your biocomputer (the brain) in a short time to bring wealth beyond your previous dreams. Relaxation is the magic key to unlocking your mind, and quickest results come with repetition. Apply this Alphamatic process at least once daily. If you wish to become wealthier in a shorter period of time, apply the Alphamatic process two, or better, three times daily:

In the morning, upon awakening... midday, after lunch... and at night, just before going to sleep.

Let me repeat: Three times daily will give quickest results!

Alphamatic Power Script

The following script can be committed to memory after reading it several times, or you may choose to take advantage of the *bonus insert* which shows you how to record on audiocassette the entire script for repeated use with your eyes closed *(for personal use only, not commercial — it is copyrighted).* Wherever the script indicates a pause, allow

five to ten seconds of silence before continuing.

First, find a quiet place where you will not
be disturbed. Sit in a comfortable chair. Place
your feet flat on the floor and your hands with
palms upward on your lap, separated from
each other.

Now... close your eyes... and take a deep
breath.

Take another deep breath, and exhale
slowly. As you exhale, relax. As you relax, imagine that your body is a large sack of gold
coins filling the chair. Feel your head, neck,
shoulders, and arms as being heavy gold
coins. Feel the weight of your hands and arms
as exceedingly heavy.

Now your whole body is a giant bag of
heavy gold coins, relaxing in the chair. To help
you relax more, imagine that in a moment, the
bottom of the sack will open, and the coins will
slide out the bottom of the sack, and onto the
floor, leaving the sack empty in the chair and
totally limp. (pause)

Now the coins are sliding from the sack.
As they slide out imagine all the tensions of
the day being released from your body. (pause)
All the coins are sliding to the floor leaving the
sack empty in the chair... and you, totally
relaxed.

Imagine a relaxing, warm, soothing light, starting at the top of your head, (pause) flowing...down into your eyes, relaxing your eyes...and then down, into your face...relaxing your face. (pause) The warm light now flows down over your cheeks, jaw and mouth areas...relaxing them. (pause) Now, allow the white light to flow down into your neck and shoulder muscles. (pause) It may feel as though someone is gently massaging the neck and shoulder areas. (pause)

Now feel the warm, relaxing white light flowing down...into your arms, elbows, and forearms. (pause) Feel the tension and energy flowing down...into your hands, and out your fingers. (pause) Feel and imagine the tingling sensation of your fingers. (pause)

Start again at your neck and shoulders, feel and imagine the gentle massaging of the light, relaxing the muscles in these areas. (pause) Feel the light flowing down...relaxing your chest area. (pause) Take a deep breath. (pause) Exhale slowly, and relax. (pause)

As the breath flows from your chest area, feel your body relax. (pause) Now feel the relaxing light flow down...into your stomach, (pause) down into your hips, (pause) down into your feet, (pause) and out your toes. (pause) Relax. (pause) Feel the tingling in the soles of your feet. (pause) Your toes are relaxed. (pause)

Now you are at a relaxed, wealthier level of mind. (pause) At this wealthy level of mind you can enjoy and know all the wealth you deserve. (pause) At this level you may review the *Power Phrases* for wealth and ever-increasing wealth.

- I Think Wealthy, Therefore I Am Wealthy.
- I Deserve To Be Wealthy.
- I Deserve And Enjoy My Wealth.
- Every Day I Become More Successful In ~~In~~ ALL Money Matters.
- I Always Look And Feel Wealthy.
- I Take A Little Extra Time In Grooming And It Always Pays Me Richly.
- I Always Have More Than I Need.
- I Pay My Bills Promptly And Joyfully With My Unlimited Supply Of Money.
- I Always Receive Great Value For My Money.
- Wealth Is Mine, Now That I Have Set My Success Destinations.
- I Enjoy My Life And My Wealth, For My Funds Are Unlimited.
- I Have Unlimited Funds In My Universal Bank Account.

- I Have An Abundance Of Creative Ideas Which Make Me Wealthier Each Day.
- Every Investment I Make Will Be Successful.
- I Make Money Every Minute Of The Day Or Night, Even While I Sleep.
- I Live In A World Of Lavish Abundance That I Deserve.
- Every Day I Am Improving My Self-Worth, Both Mentally And Financially.
- It Is Okay For Me To Have Everything I Desire.
- Every Day I Have Increasing Confidence In My Money Dealings.
- The Time For Me To Become Wealthier — Is NOW.

(pause)

Take the time to imagine what you will do with your new wealth. See yourself and your loved ones enjoying the fruits of your wealth. (pause, one minute)

Relax. (pause) Now imagine your future successes; imagine your future goals completed: (pause)

Your one month goal. (pause for thirty seconds)

Relax. (pause) Your six month goal. (pause thirty seconds)

Relax. (pause) Your one year goal. (pause thirty seconds)

Relax... and enjoy. (pause)

Every day in every way, you are becoming wealthier and wealthier. (pause)

Each time you enter these Alphamatic levels, you will increase your talents, your health, and your wealth. (pause) Your honest and loving and giving nature will bring increasing abundance in all things you desire.

Now it is time to return to the present. (pause) Feel your body becoming alert. Feel rested as if you have had a perfect night's sleep. Open your eyes now, and enjoy the world around you. Smile. Smile at yourself, smile at the world.

How To Make An Alphamatic Audiocassette

1. Purchase a quality audiocassette (C-30), thirty minutes long (fifteen minutes each side). Buy Maxell or a better quality Scotch or Memorex tape. A good quality tape is a wise investment, because you will be playing this tape repeatedly.

2. Clean your tape recorder's heads and drive wheels with cotton swabs and 190 proof alcohol. Do not use rubbing alcohol because it contains silicon which coats and causes damage to recording and playing heads.

3. When you play back your tape, do not be distressed by the sound of your voice. I have never heard of a non-professional who liked the sound of his/her voice on a home recorder. After you play it a few times, you will become accustomed to your special sound, and find it relaxing.

4. To get the full quality sound of the big studios, the great secret is to *record in your bathroom.* Remove all towels and the shower curtain. The sound bouncing off the tile creates a slight echo effect, adds fullness to your recorded voice. Record late at night when everyone is asleep. If possible, use a hand microphone to reduce mechanical noise from the tape recorder. You can buy an inexpensive tape recorder mike for less than ten dollars.

5. Read the complete script aloud at least three times before making your first recording.

6. Relax by running through the Alphamatic method in your mind before you record. Take three deep breaths... record.

7. Allow the tape to run about ten seconds before you talk. This will allow time for the

tape-leader, and will give you time to return to your chair and to relax.

8. Take your time. Speak slowly and distinctly.

9. Some will suggest using relaxing music in the background, such as *Tuning the Rainbow* or *Charging the Body Electric* or *Transformations* available from this Publisher.

For those who don't have time to make their tapes, I made one with the Alphamatic "Think Wealth" Power Phrases. It also includes, on side B, subliminal "Think Wealthy" suggestions embedded in the background ocean sound. The second tape in the kit contains a mini-seminar and my Changing of the Past Exercise used by psychologist to help rid their clients of negative memories. This Think Money Action Kit (two audio cassettes, handbook and Alphamatic card) is available at better bookstores, or from the Publisher for $14.95 plus shipping.

Your Invitation To Join
The Select Successful Group...
JOIN THE C.I.A.

It is very easy to have money confidence,
once you develop the proper attitude and
image... and if you join a select group, the
C.I.A. not the government organization, but a
Success Group.

Do you qualify for membership in the
C.I.A.?

That is, are you willing to make the necessary:

Changes in your
Images and
Attitudes?

How To Join The C.I.A.

You join this Success Group when you say and image the Alphamatics. However, membership in the C.I.A. is by *R.S.V.P.* only:

R — Read books suggested throughout this manual. Most are available from the public library or can be ordered through this Publisher. (A person who doesn't read is no better than a person who can't read.)

S — Study the concepts in these books until they are part of your belief system. It is not enough to read — you need to *study*. Review your plan at your relaxed level of mind.

V — Visualize yourself with Alphamatic energy, with the money you deserve. Remember... what you see/visualize is what you get. Use your seven steps to visualization to expand your comfort zone to embrace more of life. Go for the gold!!

P — Persist. The Twelfth Commandment: "Thou shalt be persistent in thy wealthy thinking."

Now It's Up To You!
It is your responsibility — Reread this book.... Think about it.... Work on it — and REAP!

Put Your MIND Where Your MONEY Is...
and THINK WEALTHY!

BIBLIOGRAPHY

Allen, James and Dr. Tag Powell. *As You Thinketh.* Top Of The Mountain Publishing, Florida.

Bach, Richard. *Illusions.* Dell Publishing, New York.

Clark, Glenn. *The Man Who Tapped The Secrets of the Universe.* The University of Science & Philosophy, Virginia.

Givens, Charles. Any book by this author is good.

Hadsell, Helene. *Contesting: The Name It And Claim It Game.* Top Of The Mountain Publishing, Florida.

Hill, Napoleon. *Think and Grow Rich.* Fawcett Publications, Inc., Connecticut.

Molloy, John T. *Live For Success.* Morrow & Company, New York.

Molloy, John T. *The NEW Dress For Success for Men.* Warner Books, New York.

Molloy, John T. *Women's Dress For Success.* Warner Books, New York.

Ogilvy, David. *Confessions of an Advertising Man*. Ballantine Books, New York.

Ponder, Catherine. *The Prosperity Secret For The Ages*. Unity Books, Missouri.

Powell, Dr. Tag. *Money and You*. Top Of The Mountain Publishing, Florida.

Powell, Dr. Tag and Dr. Judith L. Powell. *Silva Mind Mastery For The 90's*. Top Of The Mountain Publishing, Florida.

Selye, Hans, M.D. *Stress Without Distress*. Signet Books, New York.

Selye, Hans, M.D. *The Stress Of Life*. McGraw Hill, New York.

Speller, Jon. *Seed Money In Action*. Morning Star Press, New York.

Wattles, Wallace. *The Science of Being Great*. Top Of The Mountain Publishing, Florida.

Wattles, Wallace. *The Science of Getting Rich*. Top Of The Mountain Publishing, Florida.

DR. TAG POWELL

Dr. Tag Powell is a living example of what he preaches: That by learning to scientifically train and channel more of your mind, you can become a happier, wealthier, and more successful person.

For over a decade, Dr. Powell has expertly guided thousands along this path to excellence through a world renowned Human Potential training, and through his own highly successful Life Improvement Seminars in major cities from coast-to-coast and worldwide.

As a lecturer, he has achieved numerous awards and honors, including the Silva Method's Presidents Cup as the Best Lecturer in the United States. He has been honored with more awards in the Silva Method arena than any other lecturer in their history. Some of his other awards include: Best Educational TV Series, "Cable Spotlight Achievement Award" for "It's All In Your Mind"; Runner-up Publishers Marketing Association's "Benjamin Franklin Award" for Best Audio, at the American Booksellers Association Convention for *Speed Learning.*

Dr. Powell is the author of a number of books, including: the best-seller, *Money and You;* and co-author of the award- winning Best New Age book, *Silva Mind Mastery For The 90's* translated into nine languages; the updated and illustrated James Allen Classic, *As You Thinketh*; and *Slash Your Mortgage In Half.* He is also the Director of Powell Productions, in Largo, Florida, which produces video - audio cassettes, TV shows, Seminars and educational tours. Tag is co-director of Powell Travel Consultants, a full service travel agency.

Tag Powell earned his doctorate in Psychorientology from The Institute of Psych orientology, Texas. It is the field's highest level of certification. He also trained with Dr. O. Carl Simonton, M.D., a specialist in the field in helping cancer patients with the use of mental processing and visualization. Dr.

Powell also earned his Master certification in Neuro Linguistic Programming (NLP) from The Society of Neuro Linguistic Programming through The Southern Institute of NLP.

A favorite for radio and TV talk shows around the world, Tag's wit and humor also add zest to his lectures and seminars. At one point in his earlier career, he was a recognized New York actor and comedian. His diverse background also comprises business management, a stint as President of an advertising agency with Johnson & Johnson and Rutgers University as accounts, and even a designer of rockets.

Nine of Dr. Powell's past fourteen years as an outstanding Mind Development lecturer have been spent with Dr. Judith L. Powell, his wife and partner, and also an award-winning lecturer/writer.

Tag writes two monthly columns and numerous articles that are published in national and international magazines. Extremely innovative, he developed a subliminal system for audiocassettes with subliminals in English, Japanese and Chinese including business subliminals for a Japanese corporation. As well as Subitones, a new musical tonal process which involks a specific feeling or emotion. The Sublitone music contain NO hidden words, the tonal arrangement trigger a a specific positive responce in the brain.

Recently he conducted trainings at the University of Hong Kong and at the Malaysian Institute of Management. When they are not traveling and lecturing around the world, Tag and Judi enjoy their home in Saint. Petersburg, Florida with their Scottish Terriers, Master, Buddha and Isis.

IDEAS TO HELP YOU THINK WEALTHY...

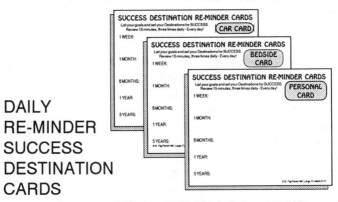

DAILY RE-MINDER SUCCESS DESTINATION CARDS

18 cards (6 months supply) to daily review and update your goals. Positive motivational poems on the back of each card. $3.50

RUBBER STAMP WITH SMILE FACE

Put FUN back into bill paying! Stamp all your checks and letters with a Smile...and program for your increased riches at the same time.

$6.95

THINK WEALTH ALPHAMATIC CARDS

18 cards (2x3.5 inch) in vinyl pocket case. Carry it in your pocket or purse to easily program yourself during the day. You are what you think...so Put Your Money Where Your Mind Is! $4.50

RELAXING BACKGROUND MUSIC

TUNING THE RAINBOW -- MUSIC
by Peter Abood and Dr. Tag Powell

A beautiful blend of harmonics and gentle persuasion, *Tuning the Rainbow* helps produce the feeling of Security and Peace, Relaxation, Freedom from Stress, and, best of all, Love. Designed to open the seven transforming energy centers (chakras) of the body. Play any time you are under stress, are feeling anger or resentment, or simply want to relax.
Contains Sublitones. No subliminally hidden words.
ISBN 0-914295-72-1, one audiocassette   US$9.95

CHARGING THE BODY ELECTRIC-MUSIC
by Peter Abood and Dr. Tag Powell

When you are feeling down, experiencing some depression, or just have the "blahs", *Charging the Body Electric* will give you Courage and Strength to carry on, build your Pride, and restore your Self-Confidence. An opportune time to listen is in your car; on your way to the office to face a hard day; in the morning, when you are getting ready to make the day's sales the best ever; or whenever you need a lift.
Contains Sublitones. No subliminally hidden words.
ISBN 0-914295-73-X, one audiocassette   US$9.95

JAZZ UP YOUR LIFE -- MUSIC
by Peter Abood and Dr. Tag Powell

Play any time you need added Energy, Happiness, Enthusiasm or Stamina to get the job done. An ideal time to listen is when you are jogging or exercising, and you need more energy to burn; while you are engaged in a hobby, and need some enthusiasm to finish; when you get home exhausted, but need stamina to get through the rest of the evening; when you're feeling down, and need a mental lift.
Contains Sublitones. No subliminally hidden words.
ISBN 0-914295-74-8, one audiocassette   US$9.95

HOW TO WIN CONTESTS AND SWEEPSTAKES

CONTESTING:

THE NAME IT AND CLAIM IT GAME

Helene Hadsell, who is called by *Family Circle Magazine* "The woman who wins every contest prize she desires," shares her winning secrets in a manner vibrant, warm and folksy that is unique to only her.

Helene will cover the secrets of how to be a winner, and how to visualize your good luck. Her use of metaphors from her experiences will help you clearly understand the principles of winning. You will learn the true secrets of why Ms. Hadsell has been one of the greatest contest winners of all time. And how she continues to win even today. Get the winning edge!

Learn the nuts and bolts information of contesting: from how to save money on envelopes; how to create a winning entry — to how to win at the exciting game of life; with sections on building a confident, creative attitude in children by showing them how to use their creative minds to win contests.

You will enjoy Helene's personal thoughts on picking that winning lottery number, and how to build the Hadsell Answer Chest — a unique decision-making tool you can develop yourself.

256-page, Illustrated Trade Paperback
ISBN 0-914295-66-7 $9.95

You will
also enjoy

AS YOU THINKETH

The James Allen Classic brought into the '90s with a total revision and rewriting by award-winning, world-class motivational trainer, Dr. Tag Powell. Many call *As You Thinketh* the *"Handbook for Higher Living,"* for it holds the true answers for enjoyment of life and successful living, others call it *The Book of Vibrant Health,"* for it explains the true causes of good health, and how to obtain it, *"The Book of Instant Enlightenment,"* for it explains the real laws of the Universe, and the secrets of how to make these laws work for you. You might even call this classic work *"The Book of Answers,"* for it covers everything from how to take off weight to reaching the top of the achievement ladder; how to overcome circumstances; to increasing your vision and ideals. Apply the techniques from this book and *it will* change your life for the better.

ISBN 0-914295-69-1
104 pages, Quality Paperback $6.95

Dr. Tag Powell's THINK MONEY 2-Audiocassette Action Kit

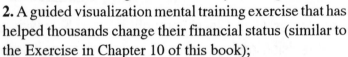

Break out of mediocrity — use your mind! Action Kit contains:
1. Mini-lecture from the famous Think Wealth Seminar taught worldwide by Dr. Tag Powell;
2. A guided visualization mental training exercise that has helped thousands change their financial status (similar to the Exercise in Chapter 10 of this book);
3. A special "Changing the Past" visualization exercise uniquely designed by Dr. Tag Powell that will help you root out the cause of your early fears or beliefs about money (psychiatrists are recommending this cassette to their patients); 4. A subliminal cassette with the powerful Alphamatics (increased wealth suggestions) embedded below the threshold of your hearing.

Kit contains two audiocassettes, handbook & Alphamatic card.   ISBN 0-914295-41-1 $14.95